VIETNAM 1939–75

SECOND EDITION

CONTENTS

1 THE JAPANESE AND FRENCH WARS

→ **Key Issue**

• Why were the French defeated?

In 1939 Vietnam was part of an area known as French Indo-China. French Indo-China consisted of Vietnam, Laos and Cambodia. The French had added these areas to their **empire** in the 19th century. French Indo-China had a population of 25 million, and 20 million of these lived in Vietnam. Indo-China was rich in natural resources. It was the world's third largest grower of rice. It also had corn, coal and rubber. Japan was keen to extend its influence in South East Asia in order to gain control of the vital raw materials Vietnam had. France's defeat in Europe in 1940 gave Japan its chance to move in on Indo-China.

INDO-CHINA OCCUPIED

In July 1941 France agreed to allow the Japanese to occupy French Indo-China mainly because they could not defend their colony against a Japanese army of 35,000 and so had no choice. The Japanese allowed the French to continue running Indo-China as long as the Japanese could take whatever resources they needed for their war against China.

The Japanese ruthlessly stripped all that they could from the region. The effect was that the local population starved. Between one and a half and two million Vietnamese starved to death in 1945. But the Vietnamese did not need to wait for an event like this in order to organise resistance to the Japanese.

THE VIETMINH

In 1941 two leading Vietnamese **communists**, Ho Chi Minh and Nguyen Vo Giap (a history teacher), set up the League for the Independence of Vietnam (or Vietminh) in southern China. Though Ho Chi Minh and Giap were communists, the Vietminh included non-communist organisations as well. The aim of the Vietminh was essentially a **nationalist** one: to establish an independent Vietnam, free from foreign domination. This meant fighting both the Japanese and the French.

HO CHI MINH

Ho was born in 1890 and was the son of a peasant. He became a school teacher but left Vietnam for Europe in 1911 as kitchen boy on a French ship. He worked as a pastry cook in a London hotel and began to get interested in politics. He then spent six years in Paris. Ho was strongly opposed to French rule in his country but he admired French culture.

He soon became a communist. At that time, communist Russia promised to assist all peoples struggling to free themselves from foreign rule. 'It was **patriotism** and not communism that originally

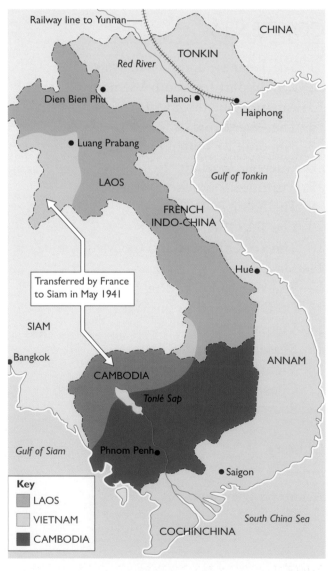

French Indo-China was a long way from France and difficult to defend against an aggressive power like Japan. The Japanese also forced France to hand over territory to Siam in 1941. Siam later became an ally of Japan.

inspired me,' he later said. In 1929 he founded the Indo-Chinese Communist Party.

AMERICAN HELP

The Vietminh was still operating from China. But it also had the help of the American intelligence service, the Organisation of Strategic Services (OSS). The OSS trained and equipped the Vietminh during the war. By the end of 1944 the Vietminh were ready to begin **guerrilla** operations against the Japanese and French in northern Vietnam.

Their campaign was mostly small-scale attacks against isolated French outposts but they were successful. Support for the Vietminh grew as a result and by early 1945 the Vietminh had about 5000 guerrilla fighters under the command of Nguyen Vo Giap.

THE DEFEAT OF JAPAN

The Japanese tried hard to hold on to Vietnam and in March 1945 they decided to get rid of the French altogether. French troops were disarmed or killed and French officials imprisoned. The Japanese offered to set up an independent Vietnam, totally free from French control. They appointed Bao Dai, the Emperor of Vietnam since 1925, as its leader.

But it was a pointless move. In August 1945 the Japanese surrendered and the Second World War was over. The Japanese would have to withdraw from all the countries of South East Asia under their control. The question was: who would replace the Japanese in Vietnam? Ho was determined that it would be the Vietminh and not the French.

Ho Chi Minh (centre) was an impressive leader. He led a simple, modest life and had a strong personality. He also had a shrewd grasp of politics. He realised that the Vietminh would attract less support if it was only a communist organisation. Ho, therefore, played down his communist beliefs.

The Vietminh were quick to replace the French and Japanese. They took control of Hanoi and Saigon and in September 1945 Ho announced that Vietnam was an independent and **democratic** republic. The United States was sympathetic. The Americans didn't want to see the old **colonial powers** like France back in charge. They believed that the Vietnamese and other Asian people had the right to rule themselves.

THE FRENCH RETURN

Nevertheless, by December 1945 there were 50,000 French troops in Indo-China ready to complete the task of restoring French power there. The Vietminh were not strong in the south of Vietnam and the French commander, Leclerc, claimed victory by March 1946.

In fact, Leclerc had made a classic mistake, one often made by professional soldiers when fighting an enemy which uses guerrilla tactics. The French could conquer Vietminh territory but they could not keep control of it. As soon as they moved on, the Vietminh would return to the villages. Leclerc simply did not have enough troops to hold down the areas they captured. The Americans were to face the same problem 20 years later. As one Vietminh fighter said of this time, 'We couldn't protect the villages, the French couldn't hold them.'

For a while an uneasy truce existed between the French in the south and Ho Chi Minh in the north. Ho travelled to Paris to work out an agreement but negotiations broke down. Both sides could only agree on a ceasefire.

Then, in November 1946, the French broke the ceasefire and launched a major attack against the Vietminh forces in Haiphong. The following month fighting started in Hanoi as well. The Vietminh retreated into the jungle, 100 kilometres north of Hanoi, and prepared for guerrilla war. They were heavily outnumbered to begin with and there was little fighting until 1950. The important development in this time was political and not military.

IMPACT OF THE COLD WAR

By 1950, the Americans' attitude to French rule in Vietnam was clear. The **Cold War** with the Soviet Union meant that the United States would now assist any country opposing the spread of communism. Ho Chi Minh was a communist and so the Americans would do whatever they could to help the French defeat him. In July 1950 – a month after the **Korean War** broke out – President Truman agreed to send the French supplies worth $15 million. In fact, the United States was to spend nearly $3 billion in the next four years helping the French.

COMMUNIST VICTORY IN THE EAST

The victory of Mao Zedong's communist forces in the war in China in 1949 was a great boost to the Vietminh. Mao provided his fellow communists in the jungles of northern Vietnam with essential military supplies, such as artillery. Mao's victory was another reason why the Americans' attitude to the French changed. Communism seemed about to sweep its way across South East Asia and it had to be stopped. Vietnam would be a good place to do it – especially if the French were doing the fighting.

'ELEPHANT FIGHTS GRASSHOPPER'

Ho Chi Minh liked to compare the Vietminh forces to a grasshopper fighting the French elephant. The reality was rather different because the Vietminh forces were not at all like feeble grasshoppers. By 1950 Giap commanded an army of over 100,000 men, well supplied with modern weapons and even trucks brought across the border from China. The French had 100,000 troops plus the support of 300,000 Vietnamese but these were not enough. The French were trying to control an area of 130,000 square kilometres of dense forest. It was an impossible task.

As long as the Vietminh played a waiting game, they could not be beaten. Safe in their jungle hide-outs, they would strike out on hit-and-run attacks on French patrols and then retreat back into the forests. However, in 1950 and 1951 Giap made the mistake of moving from this guerrilla war style of fighting to big attacks on well-defended French positions. In one attack, 50 kilometres north of Hanoi in January 1951, Giap lost 14,000 men, either killed or wounded, out of 20,000 Vietminh.

DIEN BIEN PHU

Giap was still determined to take on the French in a big, decisive battle. He chose a small village, Dien Bien Phu, close to the border with Laos. He knew the French would defend their position there as it would stop the Vietminh from getting into Laos for extra supplies of food. Patiently, Giap secretly assembled a vast army of 60,000 men with 200 heavy artillery guns on the high ground surrounding the French garrison of 15,000 troops.

This time, Giap did not launch a headlong attack against the French. Instead, he used his artillery to shell the French troops while his men dug tunnels to get them close to the enemy positions. This took two months. By the middle of March 1954 Giap was ready to attack. The French could not keep their troops properly supplied. On 7 May 1954 the surviving 10,000 French troops, half of them wounded, were forced to surrender. The rest were dead. Dien Bien Phu finally broke the French government's will to fight on. It knew the war was lost.

A SOURCE

A modern historian describes General Giap's preparations to attack the French at Dien Bien Phu (adapted from a history book, *Guerrilla Warfare*, R Corbett, 1986).

Giap's troops carried Chinese heavy artillery piece by piece on their backs over what the French had thought to be impassable mountains. Moreover, the airstrip, upon which the French depended to keep their troops supplied, became unusable in the first days of the Vietminh attacks. Although some supplies and reinforcements arrived by parachute, the loss of the airstrip meant the French were bound to be defeated.

B SOURCE

A modern historian describes General Giap's preparations to attack the French at Dien Bien Phu (adapted from *Vietnam – A History*, S Karnow, 1994).

An even more agonising ordeal for Giap's troops was to position the artillery and anti-aircraft guns in the hills above Dien Bien Phu. Again, with sheer muscle, the Vietminh dragged the heavy weapons up the slopes within range of the French garrison. By the middle of January, the Vietminh force numbered 50,000 men, while the French numbered 13,000.

C SOURCE

A modern historian describes General Giap's preparations to attack the French at Dien Bien Phu (from *Atlas of the Twentieth Century*, R Natkiel, 1982).

When the Vietminh did attack, in March 1954, the French had about 18,000 defenders. But Giap had an overwhelming superiority in numbers, and was well-supplied with artillery, including anti-aircraft guns. When the attack began, the airstrip could no longer be used: supplies could be parachuted in, at some risk.

D SOURCE

Vietminh forces bringing supplies to the front by bicycle during the build-up to the attack on Dien Bien Phu.

E SOURCE

The Vietminh in 1949 controlled a limited area of Vietnam. The most important areas were the ones where the most people lived. These were cities like Hanoi and Saigon and the Red River and Mekong deltas.

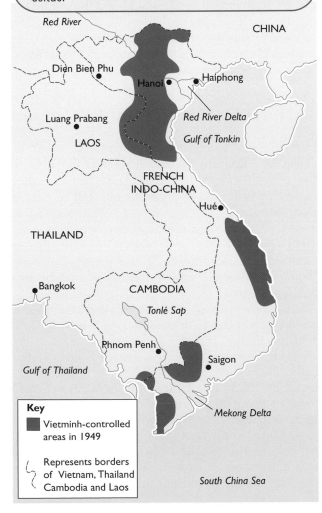

Key

Vietminh-controlled areas in 1949

Represents borders of Vietnam, Thailand Cambodia and Laos

F SOURCE

From *The Collins History of the World*, J A S Grenville, 1994.

The French discovered they could not crush the Vietminh. Their own casualties, 90,000 dead and wounded by the close of 1952, were causing increasing criticism in France. French strategy was in the hands of generals who were not the equals of General Giap.

Questions

a What can you learn from Source A about the position of the French defenders at Dien Bien Phu?

b Does Source C support the evidence of Sources A and B about the battle for Dien Bien Phu?

c How useful are Sources D and E as evidence of the strengths of the Vietminh forces?

d 'The French were defeated at Dien Bien Phu because they under-estimated the Vietminh.' Use the sources and your own knowledge to explain whether you agree with this view.

The French asked President Eisenhower of the United States to send American troops to help. There was even mention of using nuclear weapons. Eisenhower said 'no' to both. The United States had just ended the war in Korea in which over 40,000 Americans had died. The US government was in no mood to see yet more Americans die in Vietnam.

THE GENEVA AGREEMENT

The leaders of Britain, France, China, the Soviet Union, the United States, and Vietnam had already arranged to meet in May 1954 in Geneva,

CHINA

Red River

Dien Bien Phu

Hanoi

LAOS

NORTH VIETNAM

Communist North Vietnam: led by Ho Chi Minh (1946–69); backed by the Soviet Union and China

Vientiane

Gulf of Tonkin

THAILAND

Hué

17th parallel which divided Vietnam into North and South until elections planned for July 1956

Bangkok

CAMBODIA

Tonlé Sap

SOUTH VIETNAM

Phnom Penh

Saigon

Gulf of Thailand

South Vietnam: led by Ngo Dinh Diem (1955–63) who refused to hold elections in 1956; backed by the United States

Key
● Major battle

South China Sea

Vietnam after the Geneva Agreement, July 1954.

Switzerland. They met the day after Dien Bien Phu fell. Eisenhower wanted the French to carry on fighting, but they had had enough. The Vietminh wanted early elections so the people could elect a government for the whole of Vietnam. They were confident of winning. The western powers (Britain, France and the United States) wanted a long delay before elections. They were worried by Ho Chi Minh's popularity throughout Vietnam.

Eventually, the following points were agreed:
- Vietnam would be divided temporarily in two along the 17th parallel – the North under Ho Chi Minh and the South under Ngo Dinh Diem.
- The Vietminh forces would withdraw from the South and the French would pull out of the North.
- A date for the elections was fixed: July 1956.

In eight years of fighting, 400,000 soldiers and civilians had died. But few at the time believed that the Geneva Agreement really would end the conflict. For one thing, the leader of the South, Ngo Dinh Diem, refused to accept the agreement. Yet the Americans made it clear that they would support Diem because he was a strong enemy of **communism**.

THE DOMINO THEORY

Eisenhower's foreign policy followed what was called the '**domino theory**'. This was the idea that the countries of South East Asia (and elsewhere) were closely linked together. If one fell to communism, the theory was that others would also fall, like a row of dominoes. China became communist in 1949. North Korea and North Vietnam also had communist governments. If the South Vietnamese 'domino' followed, which country would be next? Malaya? Burma?

Eisenhower was determined that communism would stop at the 17th parallel (see map, left, for the 17th parallel).

Diem was 'elected' President of South Vietnam (officially called the Republic of Vietnam) in October 1955. The United States would therefore have to prop up Diem's government in the South with money, supplies and military equipment. Eisenhower knew that Diem would have to win the support of the people of South Vietnam. The fact that Diem was a Catholic while most Vietnamese were Buddhists would not make this any easier.

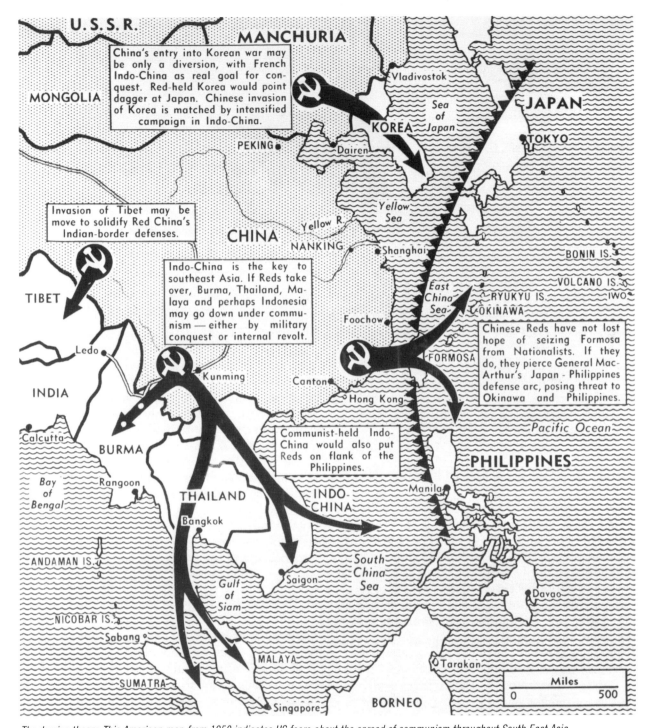

The domino theory. This American map from 1950 indicates US fears about the spread of communism throughout South East Asia.

Text labels within the map:

China's entry into Korean war may be only a diversion, with French Indo-China as real goal for conquest. Red-held Korea would point dagger at Japan. Chinese invasion of Korea is matched by intensified campaign in Indo-China.

Invasion of Tibet may be move to solidify Red China's Indian-border defenses.

Indo-China is the key to southeast Asia. If Reds take over, Burma, Thailand, Malaya and perhaps Indonesia may go down under communism — either by military conquest or internal revolt.

Chinese Reds have not lost hope of seizing Formosa from Nationalists. If they do, they pierce General MacArthur's Japan - Philippines defense arc, posing threat to Okinawa and Philippines.

Communist-held Indo-China would also put Reds on flank of the Philippines.

'DEMOCRACY' DIEM-STYLE

The statistics for Diem's election in 1955 tell a great deal about the kind of government Diem planned and the kind of man the United States was backing. Diem won with 98.2 per cent of the votes. The Americans had wisely advised him to claim only 60 or 70 per cent of the vote in his support. In Saigon there were 450,000 people entitled to vote. Somehow, 605,000 people voted for Diem! Clearly Diem had cheated in the elections.

Eisenhower hoped that Diem would carry out land reforms to help the peasants of the South get land of their own. But Diem was not interested in land reform. The minister in charge of the land reform wasn't interested either. He was a big landowner. Land abandoned by its owners during the war was taken from the peasants who were now farming it. Those few peasants who did get land had to pay for it in instalments. By contrast, when the Vietminh distributed land in the North, they gave it to the peasants.

*The Americans thought they could win over the 'hearts and minds' of the South Vietnamese by showing them the benefits of the American way of life. Somewhere down the list, after **napalm** and cluster bombs, came baseball.*

'RE-EDUCATION'

Diem was only interested in hunting down supporters of the Vietminh and 're-educating' them in prison camps. Those who couldn't be persuaded to change their views were executed. Perhaps as many as 12,000 were permanently 're-educated' in this way.

DIEM: WHO WAS THE PUPPET?

The July date for the 1956 election for the whole of Vietnam came and went. There was no election. Diem refused to allow an election in the South. Eisenhower didn't try to make him have one either. Diem knew that the United States would have to go on supporting him because he prevented a communist victory in the South. As one American official put it, Diem was 'a **puppet** who pulled his own strings – and ours as well'.

Diem's government favoured the landowners at the expense of the peasants. The landowners forced their peasant tenants to pay high taxes and even made them work for nothing at certain times of the year. The communists in the South knew that the peasants wanted to fight back. Diem's attack on the Vietminh was proving very successful. Vietminh supporters in the South were gradually being eliminated by Diem's police and army. It was time to fight back.

THE WAR BEGINS AGAIN

Eventually, in 1959, the communist government in the North issued orders to the Vietminh to begin a terror campaign against officials of Diem's government. Between 1959 and 1961, on average, 4000 South Vietnamese officials a year were assassinated by the 'Vietcong'. The term Vietcong means Vietnamese communist. The Americans decided that the government of South Vietnam should use this term rather than Vietminh. Vietminh stood for patriotism and it was bad **propaganda** for this idea to be linked to the communists in the North. The Americans thought that any phrase involving the word 'communist' was an insult.

In December 1960 the communists in Hanoi set up the National Liberation Front in the South. The NLF, though, did not consist only of communists. It had broad appeal to middle-class professionals such as doctors and teachers, as well as peasants and workers. Its main aims were to overthrow Diem, get rid of the Americans, and reunite North and South Vietnam.

A NEW PRESIDENT

A month after the NLF was created, John F Kennedy became president of the United States.

Kennedy wanted the American people to think he was tough on communism. He was keen to increase American involvement in South Vietnam but he would not send United States combat troops there. Kennedy did not want to increase the tension in the area because he was afraid that any threat to North Vietnam might bring the Chinese into the conflict to defend their fellow communists. This is what had happened during the **Korean War** when North Korea was invaded by US troops.

In a situation like this, events could get out of hand, leading even to nuclear war. Instead of sending troops Kennedy agreed to increase the number of military experts training the South Vietnamese Army, the **Army of the Republic of Vietnam (ARVN)**. These rose from 700 to 3000. By 1963 there were 16,000 of them.

A SOURCE

Adapted from *Vietnam – A History*, S Karnow, 1994.

When George Ball, a Kennedy adviser, suggested that one day there might be as many as 300,000 US troops in Vietnam, Kennedy laughed and replied, 'Well, George, you're supposed to be one of the smartest guys in town, but you're crazier than hell. That will never happen.'

B SOURCE

From *The Vietnam War, 1956–75*, A Wiest, 2002.

1967 – December: US forces in Vietnam reach 500,000.

Make brief notes under the following headings:
- The Geneva Agreement
- The domino theory
- Diem's policies
- Kennedy's worries about Vietnam.

Questions

a How did the domino theory help to bring about America's involvement in Vietnam?

b Sources A and B give different views about the extent of American involvement in Vietnam. Why do you think they are different? Use Sources A and B and your own knowledge to answer this question.

c How useful is Source C to an historian studying the effects of the war on the people of South Vietnam? Use Source C and your own knowledge to answer this question.

d Why did the United States become involved in the conflict in Vietnam? You may refer in your answer to:
- The defeat of the French
- The domino theory
- Diem's policies in South Vietnam.

Explain your answer.

C SOURCE

A group of South Vietnamese villagers wait to be evacuated after their village has been destroyed at An Hoa, November 1967.

Key Issue

- How did the South Vietnamese try stop the spread of communism?

In 1961 the United States spent nearly $270 million in military support for Diem. The **ARVN** (the South's Army of the Republic of Vietnam) numbered 170,000 troops but the number of Vietcong was estimated at just 10,000. The question the Americans should have asked themselves was: why did it take an army of 170,000 to defeat one of just 10,000?

The real point was that there wasn't a military solution to the Vietcong (VC). The only chance that Diem and the Americans had to defeat the VC was to undermine the popularity of the **communists** in the South. To do this they had to show that they could help the people as much, if not more.

THE 'STRATEGIC HAMLET' PROGRAMME

Diem's solution in 1962 to NLF popularity in the South was to take the peasants away from areas where the NLF was strong. Sympathetic villages were providing food and passing intelligence information about ARVN activities in the area to the VC. Diem's 'strategic hamlet' programme was supposed to stop the villagers helping the communists in the South. It meant moving entire village populations many kilometres away from their homes. The people were re-housed in a new location, 'protected' from the Vietcong by South Vietnamese troops.

The peasants were then told they had to pay the South Vietnamese government officials for the building materials to rebuild their homes. They even had to pay for the barbed wire to protect the houses from the VC. These items, of course, had been provided by the United States for free distribution to the Vietnamese families involved.

By the summer of 1963 over two-thirds of the population had been moved to these strategic hamlets. This system had been used successfully against communists by the British in Malaya in the 1950s. The big difference was that food was hard to come by in Malaya. In Vietnam it was easy to get hold of. The NLF did not starve. Neither were they cut off from the peasants. In many cases the NLF already had supporters inside the villages.

All that happened was that Diem had now moved communist supporters to a new area in which they could spread their ideas. Those villagers who weren't already in the NLF often became supporters because of the way they were treated. The strategic hamlet programme was a terrible failure.

'GET ON TEAM!'

The American adviser to the ARVN forces in the area, Lieutenant Colonel Vann, was angered by the failure of the ARVN commanders to work together. They squabbled with each other and, at one point, confused South Vietnamese troops ended up firing at each other. Vann quit his job. He argued that the war was being fought very badly by the South Vietnamese. The United States government was covering up the fact so as not to spoil relations with Diem.

The press in the United States was also being kept in the dark about the war at this time. Kennedy denied that there were any American troops involved in combat in Vietnam. But American jet pilots were bombing and machine-gunning NLF areas. Helicopter pilots were also transporting ARVN forces into combat zones. After a battle at Ap Bac in 1963, in which five US helicopters were shot down, an American journalist asked a military spokesman a tough question about the battle. The spokesman snapped back, 'Get on team!'

A SOURCE

A modern historian commenting on the strategic hamlet programme (from *Vietnam – A History*, S Karnow, 1994).

In reality, the strategic hamlet programme often converted peasants into Vietcong sympathisers. In many places they resented working without pay to dig moats, plant bamboo stakes and erect fences against an enemy that did not threaten them. Many were angered by corrupt officials who pocketed the money which was meant for seed, fertiliser and irrigation, as well as medical care, education and other social benefits.

B SOURCE

A modern historian commenting on the strategic hamlet programme (from *A Bright Shining Lie*, N Sheehan, 1990).

The peasants were enraged. They had seen their houses torn down or burned and had been forced to build new ones, inferior to their former homes, with their own labour and at their own expense. The local officials usually 'sold' the peasants the sheet metal roofing and other building materials provided free by the United States. They were angry at the long days of compulsory labour they had to put in digging a moat around the place, erecting the barbed wire fence, and cutting and planting sharpened bamboo stakes.

C SOURCE

A modern historian commenting on the strategic hamlet programme (from *Guerrilla Warfare*, R Corbett, 1986).

The idea was to resettle villagers in fortified enclosures, surrounded by barbed-wire fences, ditches filled with sharpened sticks, and so on ... The villagers would be given the benefits of progress – medicine, education – thus winning their 'hearts and minds'. The programme was a disaster. The strategic hamlets were little better than concentration camps.

D SOURCE

A South Vietnamese bus driver describes the action of a Vietcong assassination squad (from *Vietnam – A History*, S Karnow, 1994).

Five or six Vietcong guys stopped my bus one morning to check the identity cards of the passengers. They dragged two men off the bus and their chief said to them, 'We've been waiting for you. We've warned you many times to leave your jobs, but you haven't obeyed. So now we must carry out the sentence.'

They forced the two men to kneel by the roadside, and one of the Vietcong guys chopped off their heads with a machete. They pinned their verdicts to their shirts saying the murdered men were policemen for the South Vietnamese government. Afterwards, the Vietcong guys gave the passengers back their identity cards, saying, 'You'll get into trouble with the authorities without these.'

E SOURCE

A Vietnamese woman is held captive by an American soldier.

F SOURCE

A South Vietnamese soldier threatens a Vietcong suspect during an interrogation.

Questions

a What can you learn from Source A about the strategic hamlet programme?

b Does Source C support the evidence of Sources A and B about the strategic hamlet programme?

c How useful are Sources D and E as evidence about why the Vietcong were able to win the support of the South Vietnamese people?

d 'The South Vietnamese peasants supported the Vietcong because they were ill-treated by the government of South Vietnam.' Use the sources and your own knowledge to explain whether you agree with this view.

4 THE OVERTHROW OF DIEM

Key Issue

- Why was Diem overthrown?

DEATH BY BURNING

On 11 June 1963 a 66-year-old Buddhist monk sat down in the middle of a busy Saigon road. He crossed his legs and held his palms together in an act of prayer. Other Buddhist monks crowded round and one of them poured a can of petrol over his orange robe. The monk calmly lit a match and set himself alight. The man remained sitting for ten minutes as the flames covered his body. Eventually he toppled over. An American photographer, tipped off in advance, was there to take a photograph which stunned the world. Why had this monk, the first of seven to do this, burned himself to death?

Diem, a strong Catholic, had promoted many fellow Catholics to important jobs in the government and the army. Vietnam's Buddhists, who made up most of the population, resented this favouritism. But the real cause of their anger was Diem's anti-Buddhist policies. Buddhists, unlike Catholics, had to have government permission to carry out their acts of worship.

BUDDHIST OPPOSITION

Diem also had a law which banned all flags except the flag of Vietnam. When Catholics in Hué flew the flag of the Catholic Church the police took no action. In May 1963 the Buddhists decided to test the law by flying the Buddhist flag during celebrations of the Buddha's birthday. Troops opened fire on the celebrating crowd. Nine people were killed, eight of them children. Two days later, on 10 May, 10,000 Buddhists marched in protest. Diem ordered the arrest of leading Buddhists and their supporters.

These actions led to the suicide by burning of the Buddhist monk. The protests and the suicide got a great deal of publicity in the United States. For the first time the American media were covering stories about Diem's government and its unpopularity rather than about the war. The South

Vietnamese government claimed the monks were working for the **communists** and disregarded official American protests. Diem's sister-in-law, Madame Nhu, did not help matters when she told American officials, 'If the Buddhists wish to have another barbecue, I will be glad to supply the petrol and a match.'

THE COUP D'ÉTAT

President Kennedy realised that Diem was too unpopular to defeat the Vietcong. The government in Washington gave its approval to a plot or **coup d'état** to overthrow Diem and his brother, Nhu, who was Diem's chief adviser. There were government advisers in Washington who were worried about the coup. What if the anti-Diem plotters weren't strong enough to get rid of Diem straight away and there was a **civil war**? What if the generals who replaced Diem were no better or started fighting among themselves?

Nhu wasn't stupid. He realised that some generals were planning a coup against him and he had a plan of his own to deal with them. Unfortunately for Nhu, the general he revealed this plan to was also one of the plotters. The plotters decided, therefore, to attack before Nhu and Diem could put their plan into operation.

THE DEATH OF DIEM

The troops supporting the coup surrounded Diem's palace in Saigon on 1 November 1963. They didn't attack it. At this stage the plan was simply to force Diem and his brother to leave the country and not to kill them. The brothers managed to escape from the palace. Diem appealed to the American ambassador, Cabot Lodge, for help but none was offered. The next day they agreed to surrender on the condition that they would be allowed to leave the country. They gave themselves up.

They agreed to be taken in an armoured car for their 'protection'. A few moments later they were both shot dead. The people of Saigon cheered when they heard the news but Kennedy was stunned. An official of Diem's government summed up the situation well when he said, 'Apart from the colour of our skin, we are no different from the French.' The killing of Diem and his brother was not part of the plan. Three weeks later, Kennedy would also be dead. The general who took Diem's place lasted only three months.

THE BULLY AT THE PORCH

The new military rulers of South Vietnam tried to improve relations with all the groups Diem had treated badly or ignored, such as Buddhists, students and professional people. Buddhists were freed from prison. The government stated that its aim was a neutral South Vietnam in which the NLF would be allowed to exist. Foreign troops, eventually, would leave. This was not what the Americans wanted to hear. The new president, Lyndon Johnson, wanted to show that he was tough on communism as well.

The United States wanted a more aggressive war against the communists in Hanoi, not a 'softly softly' approach. Johnson's version of the domino theory was typically direct: 'If you let a bully come into your front yard [garden] one day, the next day he'll be up on your porch, and the day after that he'll rape your wife in your own bed.'

The United States didn't think the new government was capable of keeping the North Vietnamese 'bully' out of the neighbourhood, let alone the porch. The Americans, therefore, supported yet another coup in January 1964. The new military ruler, General Khanh, promised a more effective war against the communists. Khanh lasted a year.

A more effective war was certainly needed, and urgently. In 1957 the Vietminh had numbered just 2000. By the beginning of 1963 the number of Vietminh (or Vietcong) fighters had increased to only 23,000. But Diem's unpopular and corrupt government had encouraged a rapid growth in Vietcong support. By January 1965 there were 170,000 VC fighters operating in the South. Most of these new recruits came from the South but some were North Vietnamese Army (NVA) – trained soldiers from the North.

A SOURCE

A Buddhist monk on the government of Diem (quoted in *Vietnam – A Portrait of its People at War*, D Chanoff and D Van Thoai, 1996).

In 1955, I became aware of Diem's anti-Buddhist attitude, and it angered me. That year, the government did not allow Buddha's birthday to be celebrated as a national holiday ... I organised a demonstration ... Two miles down the road the police were waiting for us. They just cut out the front hundred or so marchers, surrounded us, and arrested us.

B SOURCE

President Eisenhower's letter to President Diem, October 1954 (adapted from the Seattle University website).

The purpose of this offer is to assist the Government of Vietnam in developing and maintaining a strong state, capable of resisting attempted [communist] aggression through military means. It hopes that such aid, combined with your own continuing efforts, will contribute effectively toward an independent Vietnam. Such a Government would, I hope, be respected at home and abroad and discourage any who might wish to impose a foreign **ideology** *[communism] on your free people.*

C SOURCE

A Buddhist monk burns himself to death in Saigon, South Vietnam, in October 1963 in protest against the policies of Diem's government.

Questions

a   Why was the United States so concerned about Diem's government?

b   Sources A and B give different views on the government of Diem. Why do you think they are different? Explain your answer using Sources A and B and your own knowledge.

c   How useful is Source C to an historian studying the opposition to Diem among the people of South Vietnam? Use Source C and your own knowledge to answer this question.

d   Why did the United States government turn against President Diem? You may refer in your answer to:
   • America's concerns about the spread of communism
   • Diem's unpopularity
   • The need for a more effective anti-communist policy in South Vietnam.

Key Issue

- Why did the United States send combat troops to Vietnam?

During the night of 31 July 1964, South Vietnamese commandos attacked North Vietnamese radar stations in the Gulf of Tonkin. The American destroyer, USS *Maddox*, assisted in the attack by monitoring the signals sent out by the radar stations. This would help to locate their positions. On the morning of 2 August three North Vietnamese torpedo boats headed straight for the *Maddox*, which was still in the area.

The *Maddox* opened fire and the torpedo boats each fired a torpedo at the American ship. Two of the torpedoes missed and the third hit the ship but didn't explode. United States jets sank one of the boats and damaged the other two. Johnson decided to play down this incident as there were no American casualties or losses. But he ordered the *Maddox* to stay in the area.

DUMB SAILORS AND FLYING FISH

During the night of 3 August the captain of the *Maddox* reported that his ship and the USS *Joy* were again being attacked by torpedoes. For four hours the two ships blasted away at an enemy they never saw. Not one sailor actually saw or heard **communist** gunfire. United States jet pilots over the 'battle' zone reported that they saw no evidence of the enemy. Johnson, this time, decided that the United States would strike back. The jet pilots changed their first reports to support the 'evidence' that there had been an attack.

There was a presidential election due in November and Johnson's **Republican** opponent had claimed that Johnson was 'soft' on communism. This incident gave the President the chance to prove the opposite. United States jets were ordered to attack North Vietnamese torpedo boat bases and about 25 of these were destroyed. In fact, Johnson knew that there had been no second attack. Two or three days later he told an official, 'Hell, those dumb, stupid sailors were just shooting at flying fish.'

Congress believed that a second attack had taken place and that North Vietnam needed to be taught a lesson. Johnson proposed 'the Gulf of Tonkin' resolution to Congress on 7 August. The resolution or law gave the President the power to take any military measures he thought necessary to defend 'freedom' in South East Asia, including South Vietnam. Johnson now had the power to escalate or step up the level of American military involvement. But he wasn't yet willing to do this. Johnson and his advisers believed that further air attacks, if needed, would be enough to bring victory.

VIETCONG ATTACKS

It soon became clear, however, that the Vietcong would prove impossible to beat by using only the South Vietnamese Army. In just two battles in December 1964 two battalions of elite, specially trained South Vietnamese troops were effectively destroyed in Vietcong ambushes. Over 700 were killed, wounded or captured – and these were the best the **ARVN** had to offer. What chance did the rest of the South Vietnamese Army stand?

United States air bases were also attacked by the NLF. In February 1965 Vietcong **guerrillas** destroyed ten American helicopters, killed eight servicemen, and wounded over 100.

A United States adviser shows a group of South Vietnamese soldiers how to use a bayonet. A frightening weapon perhaps, but the bayonet in Vietnam proved more useful for opening cans of fruit.

FLIES AND THE MANURE PILE

A week later, on 13 February, the President gave his approval to 'Operation Rolling Thunder'. The air force commander recommended bombing North Vietnam because 'we are swatting flies when we should be going after the manure pile'. The bombing began on 2 March 1964. It was a major escalation of the United States' role in the war and it was quickly followed by another. In the same month, 3500 United States combat troops arrived in Vietnam to protect the air bases being used to bomb North Vietnam. By the end of the year there would be 200,000 of them. America's war had begun.

A SOURCE

From an article written in 1994 on the Gulf of Tonkin incident (from a US website, www.fair.org).

On the night of Aug. 4, the Pentagon proclaimed that a second attack by North Vietnamese PT boats had occurred earlier that day in the Tonkin Gulf. Johnson ordered US bombers to 'retaliate' for a North Vietnamese torpedo attack that never happened.

One of the Navy pilots flying overhead that night was squadron commander James Stockdale. He said, 'I had the best seat in the house to watch that event and our destroyers were just shooting at phantom targets – there were no PT boats there … There was nothing there but black water and American fire-power.'

In 1965, Lyndon Johnson commented: 'For all I know, our Navy was shooting at whales out there.'

B SOURCE

From President Johnson's message to Congress, 5 August 1964 (from *Documents of American History*, H S Commager, 1968).

Last night I announced to the American people that the North Vietnamese regime had conducted further deliberate attacks against US naval vessels operating in international waters, and I had therefore directed air action against gunboats and supporting facilities used in these hostile opera-tions. This air action has now been carried out with substantial damage to the boats and facilities. Two US aircraft were lost in the action.

C SOURCE

Wrecked aircraft litter a US air base in South Vietnam after a Vietcong attack on 7 February 1965.

Questions

a Why did Johnson change his policy over the two Gulf of Tonkin incidents?

b Sources A and B give different views on the Gulf of Tonkin incident. Why do you think they are different? Explain your answer using Sources A and B and your own knowledge.

c How useful is Source C to an historian studying the reasons Johnson sent troops to South Vietnam in 1965? Use Source C and your own knowledge to answer the question.

d How important was the Gulf of Tonkin incident as a reason for the US sending combat troops to South Vietnam? You may refer in your answer to:
  • How the incident led to US troops being sent to South Vietnam
  • The impact of the domino theory
  • Johnson and his political opponents in the US.

Key Issue

- What tactics did each side use?

'Operation Rolling Thunder' – the American bombing campaign over North Vietnam – was supposed to last eight weeks. It lasted three and a half years. During the war, the United States Air Force dropped more bombs on North Vietnam than all the bombs dropped during the Second World War.

Some United States advisers told Johnson that Rolling Thunder would not achieve any significant results in this war either. North Vietnam had few factories to bomb. It was mostly countryside and the bombing would have little effect.

The supporters of bombing claimed that the campaign would destroy North Vietnam's supply routes to the NLF in the South. In this way, the Vietcong would soon run out of weapons and equipment. Johnson also believed that bombing would convince the North that the United States wouldn't give up and this would persuade the North to agree to a compromise.

SEARCH AND DESTROY

The strategy of General Westmoreland, the commander of the US forces, was that the American troops would search out and destroy the big enemy forces and the regular or professional troops of the North Vietnamese Army (NVA) operating in the South. This would leave the South Vietnamese troops to deal with the less well-trained **guerrilla** forces or Vietcong. Westmoreland was convinced that his troops would defeat their enemy because they were better equipped and had the benefit of artillery and air support.

Searching out and destroying the enemy was one thing. But all too often the enemy could not be found, let alone destroyed. Frustrated and frightened American troops settled on searching out villages and destroying those instead. In most cases, these villages played no role in supporting the VC. The troops came to call these operations 'Zippo' raids after the name of the lighters they used to set fire to the thatched houses of the Vietnamese villagers.

UNPOPULAR JOBS

The most unpopular jobs in an infantry platoon of 35 men were operating either the radio or the M-60 machine-gun. Both were three times heavier than a rifle and the men carrying them were certain targets in an ambush. Even though they were unpopular jobs, they were never given to inexperienced soldiers. 'Walking point' was also unpopular. It involved leading the platoon in the forest, watching for the enemy and checking for booby traps.

As you might expect, soldiers feared death and being wounded. But in some cases they feared being a coward even more. Nobody liked to show himself up in front of his buddies.

SMALL ARMS

Fifty-one per cent of Americans killed in the war were killed by small arms fire. Small arms are pistols, rifles and machine-guns – basic military equipment. It was not a war of big battles involving thousands of troops, but a war of small, deadly skirmishes or 'fire-fights', often during ambushes. These would involve only a few dozen men on each side, fighting at close range.

BOOBY TRAPS

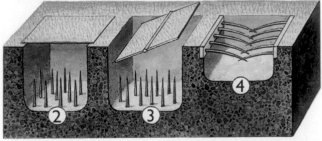

Booby traps were designed to maim or kill careless American soldiers. Punji stakes made from bamboo were dug in on the other side of a trip wire (1). Pits (2) and (3) were as deep as a man. Trap (4) was designed to snare a man's lower leg (the curved spikes made it difficult to pull the leg out).

Soldiers out on patrol didn't only have an enemy ambush to worry about. Eleven per cent of deaths were caused by booby traps. These were cheap, easy to make, and very effective. Sharpened bamboo stakes, hidden in shallow pits under sticks and leaves, could easily pierce the sole of a boot. Sometimes the spikes were smeared with human or animal excrement so the wound would be infected.

A trip wire strung across a jungle path would pull a grenade out of a tin can when it caught a soldier's leg. Soldiers wading in deep water could also catch the trip wire on such traps.

MINES

Mines were more sophisticated traps. A soldier would trigger off a 'Bouncing Betty' mine by stepping on it. The mine was fired about a metre into the air before exploding in front of the man walking behind. It was designed to explode at the same height as a man's genitals.

The casualties caused by these weapons greatly increased the tension and frustration the survivors felt because there was no enemy to be seen, no one to shoot at.

WAR FROM THE AIR

What the North Vietnamese and the Vietcong feared most were the bombing raids by American planes. The **communist** forces dug deep tunnels and used these as air-raid shelters. The tunnels around Saigon ran for 320 kilometres. Not all tunnels, though, were as well-designed as these. Some offered little protection from the effect of the bombs – at least for the men.

The Americans had developed a variety of bombs for use against the enemy. All of them caused terrible wounds. Cluster bombs were called 'mother bombs' by the Vietnamese. They exploded in the air and released up to 600 smaller bombs. When one of these hit the ground, it exploded into thousands of metal pellets.

These bombs could kill, but they were really intended to wound. A wounded enemy has to be given medical treatment. He has to be taken from the battlefield by other soldiers. All this ties up other troops and scarce medical resources. Later the pellets were made from fibre glass. These pellets did not show up in X-rays and operations were therefore much more difficult.

*A wounded **GI** being taken back for medical treatment during the battle for Hué in 1968. American and communist troops tried very hard to bring back the bodies of their dead. This was good for morale. The VC and NVA also did this because it added to the United States troops' frustration – a high 'body count' of enemy dead was a key part of the American strategy.*

NAPALM

Napalm was a bomb which exploded and showered the surrounding victims with a burning petroleum jelly. Napalm sticks to the skin and burns at 800 degrees centigrade.

THE FIRST BATTLE

The pattern of the war was quickly set. United States forces, when they came across the Vietcong, would often inflict heavy casualties on them. Air strikes proved particularly effective. In November 1965, for example, the Americans fought their first battle against NVA forces in the Ia Drang Valley. The NVA lost an estimated 1800 men during the four-day battle, compared with 240 American troops. But the North Vietnamese retreated into neutral Cambodia and the United States forces couldn't follow. Later, the NVA force reappeared in South Vietnam, after making up its losses.

General Westmoreland was pleased with the result. The 'kill ratio' was favourable: one American killed for almost eight communists. Over 33,000 American artillery shells and 7000 rockets had been fired in the battle. All this helped to convince him that the 'search and destroy' strategy was right and that superior United States fire-power would always guarantee victory in this kind of confrontation. The North Vietnamese, he believed, couldn't survive casualties like these for long. But he was wrong.

This was the big difference between the sides. The communists were so committed to their cause that they would accept these losses. Westmoreland thought that American public opinion would do the same. But he was, once again, wrong.

THE NVA – LEARNING LESSONS

The North Vietnamese also learned an important tactical lesson from the battle. In future, the regular NVA troops and Vietcong would try to avoid pitched battles with the enemy. Hit-and-run guerrilla raids and ambushes would mean fewer casualties. If they had to fight the Americans in big battles, then they would try to keep as close as they could to them during the fighting. This would make it difficult for the American troops to call in artillery fire or air strikes, since these might hit their own forces as well.

THE HO CHI MINH TRAIL

Another key element in the communist strategy was keeping their forces in the South supplied. This was achieved through the Ho Chi Minh Trail. By the end of the war, the Trail consisted of a network of 15,000 kilometres of roads through jungles and mountains. It ran from the north to the south through neutral Laos and Cambodia. There could be as many as ten different routes between two points. If one was bombed, then another could be used. Despite repeated bombing by the United States Air Force in attacks like Operation Rolling Thunder, it is likely that the North managed to get at least two-thirds of its supplies through to the South.

A SOURCE

Trinh Duc, a Vietnamese communist, describes the tactics he experienced (from *Vietnam – A Portrait of its People at War*, D Chanoff and D Van Thoai, 1996).

There was no way we could stand up to the Americans. Every time they came in force we ran from them. Then when they turned back, we'd follow them. We practically lived on top of them, so they couldn't hit us with artillery and air strikes . . .

The Americans' style was to hit us, then call for planes and artillery. Our response was to break contact and disappear if we could, but if we couldn't we'd move up right next to them so the planes couldn't get at us.

B SOURCE

From *The Vietnam War, 1956–75*, A Wiest, 2002.

The NVA and the VC began to adopt the policy of 'hanging on to American belts'. This policy called for communist fighters to get as close possible to the US forces before opening fire. If they were in close enough the US forces would avoid using their artillery and aircraft for fear of hitting their own troops.

C SOURCE

A modern historian describes the Battle of Ia Drang between the Americans and NVA in 1965 (from *Bright Shining Lie*, N Sheehan, 1990).

A pitiless struggle started, Vietnamese and Americans killing each other within yards. The close quarters deprived Moore's men of the advantage of air and artillery, and the Vietnamese did all they could to keep the killing on an infantry against infantry basis by staying as close to the Americans as possible, a tactic they called 'clinging to the belt'.

A US soldier carrying a Vietnamese woman to a helicopter to transport her out of a combat zone.

E SOURCE

One soldier wrote to his parents in April 1967 about American treatment of Vietnamese civilians (from *A Life in a Year*, J R Ebert, 1993).

We kill more civilians here per day than VC, either by accident or on purpose and that's just plain murder. I'm not surprised that there are more VC. We make more VC than we kill by the way these people are treated. I won't go into detail but some of the things that take place would make you ashamed of good old America.

F SOURCE

American troops carrying out a 'search and destroy' mission. This soldier is using his Zippo lighter to set fire to a Vietnamese peasant's home.

Questions

a What can you learn from Source A about communist combat tactics against the Americans?

b Does Source C support the evidence of Sources A and B about communist combat tactics against the Americans?

c How useful are Sources D and E as evidence of US treatment of Vietnamese civilians?

d 'The tactics used by the communist forces were more appropriate than those of the Americans for the Vietnam War.' Use the sources and your own knowledge to explain whether you agree with this view.

Make brief notes under the following headings:
- The Gulf of Tonkin Incident
- Operation Rolling Thunder
- 'Search and Destroy'
- NVA Strategy.

Americans tended to accept that the NVA were very good soldiers. They wore uniforms and fought the Americans and South Vietnamese on equal terms. But attitudes to the Vietcong were very different. They were not regular troops. They were **guerrilla** fighters. They wore the traditional, civilian black 'pyjamas' of the Vietnamese peasant and couldn't be recognised as guerrillas. The United States forces found this kind of warfare very frustrating. All the same, American troops could respect astonishing courage wherever it came from.

BODY COUNT

Westmoreland was convinced that the war would be won by killing large numbers of the enemy. This was a similar attitude to that held by generals during the First World War. The chief aim of the United States infantry was to get a high enemy 'body count'. The problem was that the NVA and VC were prepared to suffer high casualties, and the Americans always exaggerated the number of the enemy they killed anyway.

The best way to get a high body count was to send out a patrol as bait. If the NVA or VC had more men than the patrol they might attack it. The attacked patrol would then call in the air strikes or artillery fire. These tactics could cause terrible casualties but it was never easy for the Americans to be sure of the numbers. The **communist** troops tried very hard to take their dead and wounded with them. This meant that often the body count would be disappointingly low.

Neither side bothered with enemy wounded. It was too difficult to care for them and get them back for treatment. They were generally shot. Healthy prisoners had a better chance of being taken back for interrogation – and probably torture.

DEFOLIANTS

If the enemy couldn't be forced into battle, then the villages in the surrounding area became the target instead. Chemicals were sprayed in jungle areas to kill off the vegetation so that the Vietcong couldn't use the jungle for cover. But the United States also used these defoliants to destroy crops. This stopped the guerrillas getting food supplies and it also punished those villages suspected of helping the communists. On other occasions the villages were set alight.

All this was supposed to convince the peasants not to help the VC. With their crops destroyed, villagers had no choice but to re-settle in new villages away from VC-controlled areas. This, of course, made it easier for the Americans and **ARVN** to isolate the guerrillas.

The most used defoliant was Agent Orange. It was later discovered that Agent Orange contained a dioxin which caused cancer among those who used it or were affected by it. It also led to pregnant women giving birth to terribly deformed children. Traces of the chemical got washed by the rain into streams from which soldiers on both sides drank.

A SOURCE

A US soldier describes his attitude to the Vietnamese people (from *A Life in a Year*, by J R Ebert, 1993).

The way we were trained was that they were more animal than anything. You just didn't trust any of them. We were always told that kids or women were just as much your enemy as anybody else. We never trusted any of them. I already hated them before I went over there. Pretty much anything with slanted eyes was the way I was. You always thought they were snakes – sneaky, which they are. Slant-eyed people, you couldn't trust them.

B SOURCE

A US soldier writing to his parents from South Vietnam in 1968 (from *The Bloody Game*, edited by P Fussell, 1992).

I am now filled with both respect and hate for the VC and the Vietnamese. Respect because the enemy knows that he can't stand up to us in a fire fight due to our superior training, equipment and our vast arsenal of weapons. Yet he is able. I've developed hate for the Vietnamese because they come around selling Coke and beer to us and then run back and tell the VC how many we are, where our positions are, and where the leaders position themselves.

C SOURCE

An American soldier describes his attitude to the enemy (from *A Life in a Year*, by J R Ebert, 1993).

I could respect the NVA. They put on the uniform and they came at you head-on. I never believed that there was honour between warriors on opposite sides of the battle, but I see that there is. But dealing with the Vietcong was real hard because they didn't stand up and fight like men. It was real easy for me to dehumanise the Vietcong.

D SOURCE

This wounded VC guerrilla is being looked after by United States troops. Terribly wounded in the stomach, he had carried his intestines around with him for three days in a bowl. When he asked for a drink, the South Vietnamese interpreter refused. An angry American soldier offered the Vietcong his canteen instead, saying, 'Any soldier who can fight for three days with his insides out can drink from my canteen anytime.'

E SOURCE

Varnado Simpson, one of the members of Charlie Company at My Lai, describes his experience in Vietnam (from *Four Hours in My Lai*, Michael Bilton and Kevin Sim, 1989).

That day in My Lai, I was personally responsible for killing about 25 people. Personally. Men, women. From shooting them, to cutting their throats, scalping them, to ... cutting off their hands and cutting out their tongue. I did it ... I just went. My mind just went. And I wasn't the only one that did it. A lot of other people did it. I just killed. Once I started, the ... training, the whole programming part of killing, it just came out.

F SOURCE

A dead NVA soldier.

Questions

a What can you learn from Source A about how US troops were trained to see the Vietnamese?

b Does Source C support Sources A and B about US attitudes towards the enemy?

c How useful are Sources D and E as evidence of the attitudes of US troops towards the enemy?

d 'The American soldiers hated the enemy.' Use the sources and your own knowledge to explain whether you agree with this view.

8 THE SOLDIERS' WAR

Key Issue

- What was it like to fight in Vietnam?

STATISTICS

Around 2.8 million Americans served in Vietnam. Two million of them were **drafted** or **conscripted**. But only about ten per cent of these were likely to see any combat. In a typical 12-month tour of duty, the average **GI** (United States soldier) stood a two per cent chance of being killed and a ten per cent chance of getting seriously wounded. The casualty rate is much higher, though, if you consider only those who took part in actual combat.

Of all those killed in combat, 43 per cent died in the first three months of their tour of duty. Only six per cent of deaths took place among soldiers in their last three months. In total, 58,000 were killed. Their average age was 19. If you were white, wealthy and well educated you stood a much better chance of not being drafted. Those who had places at university could have their call-up delayed until after their degree. For this reason, blacks, Hispanics (Americans of Mexican descent) and poor whites made up the majority of the infantry in Vietnam.

Most of the men who arrived in the very early stages of the war were professional soldiers. The army was their chosen career. They were motivated and committed. By 1967, however, most of the arrivals had been drafted. Very few believed that they were defending democracy or even cared. Their only aim was to count the day to DEROS (Date Eligible for Return from Overseas).

TRAINING: 'KILL A GOOK EVERY DAY'

The Americans were trained to see their enemy as less than human. This made it easier to kill them. Slang terms for the NVA, Vietcong or even just the Vietnamese were an important part of this. 'Gook', 'dink' and 'slope' (from the shape of the eyes of the Vietnamese) were common terms.

'CHERRIES'

Westmoreland hoped that the one-year tour of duty system would keep up morale. This was probably not true. The constant supply of replacements undermined morale. Replacements were the new arrivals, brought in to replace men who had been killed or severely wounded. It wasn't easy joining a group of men who had been buddies for many months and had seen combat together. It would take a few weeks before replacements, known as 'cherries', would be accepted. Cherries made mistakes, and on a patrol a mistake could cost the lives of other men. Most would not be accepted until they had been tested under combat conditions.

'FRAGGING'

The men in each platoon found it difficult to get to know each other and to work as a unit. No sooner had the men learned the skills of survival and combat than it was time for them to leave. Soldiers getting close to the end of their tour (being 'short') were desperate to avoid combat or risks. This made them less effective. One commentator wrote that 'America did not fight a ten-year war, it fought a one-year war ten times'. The one-year tour of duty system probably greatly reduced the fighting efficiency of the American army.

Relations between officers and conscripted soldiers could become very difficult. Many officers were career soldiers. They wanted promotion and needed a successful combat record with a high body count of enemy 'kills'. Most of the ordinary GIs simply wanted to stay alive until their DEROS. Hostility towards these officers sometimes led the men to kill them. 'Fragging' was the term used to describe the killing of an officer by his own men. The estimate is that three per cent of all officers who died in Vietnam were killed by their own troops. During 1970 and 1971 there were over 700 cases of fragging in the United States army – and this was when there were fewer troops in Vietnam.

DRUGS

Drug-taking further reduced the effectiveness of United States forces in Vietnam. Marijuana was the most popular drug. GIs would smoke it in base camp and during 'R and R' (Rest and Recreation, a period of leave away from the front line). Cocaine and heroin were also used. Amphetamines were used to keep troops awake during night-time ambushes and just to get 'high'. In 1971, 5000 men were treated in hospital for combat wounds and 20,000 were treated for drug abuse.

WHAT WAS US MORALE LIKE?

The fact that American troops used drugs and sometimes 'fragged' their own officers is evidence of their low morale. Other factors can also lead to low morale. Soldiers need to believe that the cause they are fighting for is a good one. They also need to believe that the people back home support the war and their part in it. If they believe the cause isn't good or that they're not supported, then troops quickly lose heart. Between 1966 and 1973 there were 503,000 incidents of **desertion** in the American army in Vietnam. It should be pointed out, though, that this doesn't mean that 503,000 different soldiers deserted, as some soldiers would desert more than once, and the figure includes **draft-dodgers**.

The morale of American troops seemed to be good in the early stages of the war. This may have been because most of these men were full-time, career soldiers and had volunteered. As the war went on, more and more of the troops were conscripted. Many men simply wanted to return home.

A SOURCE

An officer in the North Vietnamese Army (from *Vietnam – A Portrait of its People at War*, D Chanoff and D Van Thoai, 1996).

We had such hatred for the enemy and such devotion to the noble cause of liberating our oppressed people that we felt we could overcome any difficulty and make any sacrifice. We were defending our country and our people and punishing the aggressors. The point is that we had faith in the cause we were fighting for, and that this faith was reinforced by effective propaganda.

B SOURCE

President Johnson's speech to Congress in August 1964 (adapted from *Documents of American History*, H S Commager, 1968).

The threat to the free nations of South East Asia has long been clear. The North Vietnamese regime has constantly tried to take over South Vietnam and Laos. As president of the United States I have decided that I should now ask the Congress to join me in making clear that all such attacks will be opposed, and that the United States will continue in its basic policy of assisting the free nations of the area to defend their freedom.

C SOURCE

Communist forces bringing supplies from North Vietnam to the South.

Questions

a What were the weaknesses in America's conscription policy?

b Sources A and B give different views about the war in Vietnam. Why do you think they are different? Use Sources A and B and your own knowledge to answer this question.

d How useful is Source C to an historian studying how the Vietcong were kept supplied during the war? Use Source C and your own knowledge to answer this question.

d How good was the morale of US troops in Vietnam? You may refer in your answer to:
- Conscription
- 'Fragging'
- Drug abuse
- Motivation.

9 THE TET OFFENSIVE, 1968

Key Issue

- Who won the Tet Offensive?

On 31 January 1968 70,000 Vietcong launched a massive attack on 100 towns and cities in South Vietnam. It was launched during the Vietnamese New Year or Tet holiday. The Americans and South Vietnamese were taken by surprise because half of the **ARVN** (South Vietnamese Army) were on leave for the Tet holiday. For the first time, the war came right into the cities. It was a war neither side was used to fighting. The Vietcong abandoned the **guerrilla** war style of fighting. Instead, they took on the United States and ARVN forces in a series of conventional battles.

This city war was also one which the VC were not equipped to fight. They found themselves forced to hold positions that they couldn't really defend. In the jungle they would simply have melted away. There they always avoided fighting battles where the odds were against them. In the Tet Offensive they couldn't do this and paid the penalty.

AIMS OF THE TET OFFENSIVE

The **communist** government in Hanoi had important political objectives for the offensive. They hoped that the local South Vietnamese population would rise up in support and help them overthrow the Saigon government. They also hoped that the United States would realise that they couldn't win the war and so begin to withdraw their forces. If nothing else happened, this at least would leave the South Vietnamese on their own.

There's no doubting the dramatic impact the attacks had on United States and world opinion. One of the most remarkable events was the attack by a 15-man suicide squad of VC guerrillas who fought their way into the American embassy in Saigon. They held out for six hours before being killed. American television showed film of the attack to 50 million homes in the United States. The American public was astonished by what they saw. The embassy was the symbol of the American presence in Vietnam and it wasn't safe from the enemy. If the embassy couldn't be defended, then what

could? American public opinion quickly began to turn against the war.

HORROR IN HUÉ

The National Liberation Front or communist forces (NLF) also attacked Hué, a major city further north. They held it for 25 days until ARVN and United States forces recaptured the city. Before this could take place, though, the VC executed about 3000 civilians. Their 'crime' was that they had links with the South Vietnamese government as officials or army officers. Basically, they killed anyone they considered hostile to the NLF. The NLF had taken its chance to get rid of a large number of its enemies. This massacre helped the case of those in the United States and Saigon who claimed that many thousands more would die if the communists won. This is why the war had to go on.

MILITARY CONSEQUENCES

In military terms, the Tet Offensive (which lasted less than a month) was a disaster for the Vietcong or NLF. Most of the 45,000 fighters killed were from the NLF and only a minority were from the North Vietnamese Army. American deaths came to 1500 and the ARVN lost 3000 dead. There were about 14,000 civilians killed. The offensive destroyed many of the finest fighters the Vietcong had and wiped out the NLF's organisation in the South.

These experienced southern communist leaders had to be replaced by men sent from the North. This meant that now the NLF was firmly under the control of the government in Hanoi. The NLF had finally lost its independence as a guerrilla organisation. Many resented the control of these northerners over 'their' movement.

A SOURCE

A modern historian on the Tet Offensive (from *The Vietnam War, 1956–75*, A Wiest, 2002).

The Tet Offensive had been a total failure for the communists. Of the 84,000 troops committed to Tet, nearly 58,000 had been killed, almost wiping out the Vietcong as an effective fighting force. The communists had expected that the ARVN would crumble, but it had fought hard and well. Tet had been a rash and demoralising defeat but surprisingly it would also turn the tide of the war in favour of the communists.

B SOURCE

A modern historian on the Tet Offensive (from *The USA and Vietnam, 1945–75*, V Sanders, 2002).

The North Vietnamese government dreamed that their great offensive would cause the government of South Vietnam to collapse. At the very least it hoped to demonstrate such strength that America would give up. The Tet Offensive was one of those rare battles lost by both sides. The communists had suffered serious losses.

C SOURCE

A modern historian on the Tet Offensive (from *Guerrilla Warfare*, R Corbett, 1986).

While Tet weakened the communists militarily, the overall consequences were without doubt favourable to the North. The over-optimistic communist leaders who had expected the South Vietnamese government to collapse had been proved wrong, but the more cautious strategists who had hoped to weaken the Americans' will to fight were encouraged by the effects of Tet.

D SOURCE

A group of US troops shelter from enemy fire behind a tank during the Tet Offensive.

E SOURCE

Huong Van Ba was an artillery officer in the NVA. He was involved in the Tet Offensive and told this to his American interviewer (from *Vietnam – A Portrait of its People at War*, D Chanoff and D Van Thoai, 1996).

When the Tet campaign was over, we didn't have enough men left to fight a major battle, only enough to make hit-and-run attacks on posts. So many men had been killed that morale was very low. We spent a great deal of time hiding in tunnels, trying to avoid being captured. We experienced many desertions. We heard that in the North there were more young people trying to avoid the draft.

F SOURCE

A map showing the Vietcong attacks during the Tet Offensive.

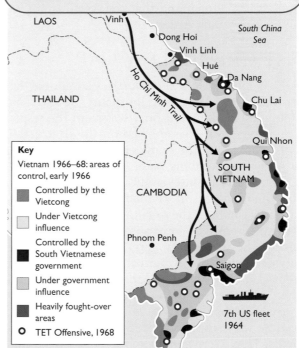

Questions

a What can you learn from Source A about the Tet Offensive?

b Does Source C support the evidence of Sources A and B about the Tet Offensive?

c How useful are Sources D and E as evidence about the Tet Offensive?

d 'The Tet Offensive was a disaster for the communists.' Use the sources and your own knowledge to explain whether you agree with this view.

Key Issue

- Did the media affect the war's outcome?

To begin with, the American newspaper and television journalists (the media) were in favour of the war. The chief editor of *Life* magazine in 1965 wrote that 'the war is worth winning'. Gradually, though, attitudes began to change. Two years later, in October 1967, that same editor wrote that the United States was not really threatened by the communists in Vietnam and that the war was not worth the lives of young Americans.

THE CREDIBILITY GAP

In December 1966 the North Vietnamese finally permitted an American journalist to visit North Vietnam. Harrison Salisbury was from the respected *New York Times*. He reported on the destruction to civilian areas and the many civilian casualties caused by American bombing raids.

The United States military had always denied that their bombs hit civilian targets. If there were civilian casualties, they claimed, then there weren't many of them. The journalist's reports widened still further the 'credibility gap'. This is the difference between what the American military and government said and what the American people believed. The wider the gap, the less the people believed.

By 1968 the United States military in Vietnam had become very suspicious of the role of the American media. They were convinced that they were turning public opinion in the United States against a war that the American and South Vietnamese forces were winning. The commander of the forces in Vietnam, General Westmoreland, had claimed in 1967 that he could see the light of victory at the end of the tunnel.

It is more likely that journalists were only reflecting a change of opinion among the people of the United States. In August 1967, for the first time, an opinion poll showed that more Americans (46 per cent) thought the war was a 'mistake' than those who thought it was right (44 per cent). It is worth pointing out, though, that this poll was taken just after President Johnson had announced an increase in taxes to pay for the war. The war was costing Americans $20 billion a year at this time.

THE IMPACT OF TET

The news film of the Tet Offensive had a dramatic effect. Especially stunning was film of the Vietcong **guerrillas** fighting in the grounds of the United States embassy. Walter Cronkite, America's most respected television journalist, saw the news film. 'What the hell is going on? I thought we were winning this war,' he said. Cronkite's opinion would influence millions of Americans. 'If I've lost Walter, I've lost Mr Average Citizen,' President Johnson said. He decided not to stand for re-election as president in 1968.

The next day saw the most dramatic television film of the offensive and perhaps the war. An American news cameraman filmed a tied-up VC suspect being led by a group of **ARVN** troops. As he was filming, the Chief of the Saigon Police walked up to the suspect and took out his pistol. He shot him once in the head. The VC suspect collapsed, a fountain of blood gushing from the side of his head.

To American viewers, the incident was shocking. The Chief of Police had clearly shot the man without a trial, on the spot, and not in self-defence. To them the victim was just a man wearing a checked shirt and shorts. In fact, it was discovered later that the victim was a member of a VC assassination squad which had been killing opponents of the communists in Saigon. At the time, though, it just looked like a brutal execution. Was this the sort of behaviour the United States was defending in Vietnam?

A 15-man VC suicide squad fought its way into the American embassy in Saigon. Within six hours they were all dead, like the ones shown here. But the political effect of this daring attack was much more important than the military result.

A SOURCE

General Westmoreland commanded the United States forces in Vietnam until June 1968. In 1979 he gave his views on the role of the American media in the war.

Actions by opponents of the war in the United States were supported by the news media. The media, no doubt, helped to back up the message that the war was 'illegal' and 'immoral' . . .

Then came the enemy's Tet Offensive of early 1968. The North Vietnamese and the Vietcong suffered such a military defeat that it took them four years to recover. Despite this, reporting of the Offensive by press and television in the United States gave an impression of an endless war that could never be won.

B SOURCE

A modern historian on the role of the media during the war (from *Vietnam – A History*, S Kamow, 1994).

But public opinion surveys conducted at the time made it plain that the Tet episode scarcely altered American attitudes toward the war.

Public 'support' for the war had been slipping steadily for two years before Tet. This was a trend caused by the increasing casualties, rising taxes and, especially, the feeling that there was no end in view. For a brief moment after the Tet Offensive began, Americans rallied behind the flag in a predictable display of patriotic fervour. But their mood of despair quickly returned as the fighting dragged on, and their support for the conflict continued to fall.

Questions

a To what extent did the communists achieve their aims for the Tet Offensive?

b Sources A and B give different views of the role of the US media during the Tet Offensive. Why do you think they are different? Use Sources A and B and your own knowledge to answer this question.

c How useful is Source C to an historian studying the Tet Offensive? Use Source C and your own knowledge to answer this question.

d 'The United States were clearly losing the war by early 1968.' Do you agree? You may refer in your answer to:
- Why the US entered the war
- How successful US tactics were
- The impact of the Tet Offensive.

Make brief notes under the following headings:
- US conscription policy
- The Tet Offensive: aims
- The Tet Offensive: results
- The Tet Offensive and the US media.

C SOURCE

The execution of a Vietcong suspect by the Saigon Chief of Police during the Tet Offensive.

11 MY LAI

Key Issue

- How did My Lai affect the United States?

On 16 March 1968, just south of Khe Sanh, an American patrol approached a small village called My Lai. The battle for Khe Sanh, where a US base was under siege, and the Tet Offensive were still raging and the village was in an area controlled by the Vietcong. Lieutenant Calley and his platoon, searching for VC, entered the village. They found no VC and did not come under enemy fire.

Instead, they then committed the worst atrocity reported of American troops throughout the war. An American investigation into the massacre later reported that 347 men, women, children and babies were murdered. Other reports put the number of dead at over 500. Some of the women had been raped first. One soldier later admitted killing babies clinging to their mothers' bodies because, he said, the babies were about to attack.

A US pilot, Hugh Thompson, witnessed the massacre from his helicopter. He was enraged by what he saw and landed his helicopter, giving orders to the gunner to open fire on any soldiers who shot at civilians. He rescued nine civilians, including five children, and flew them back to hospital.

IMPACT OF MY LAI

News of the massacre was kept quiet. Officially, the operation at My Lai had been a success. United States troops had killed 90 VC fighters, according to the company commander's report. The only casualty the Americans had was one soldier shot in the foot. This soldier later said he had shot himself to get out of the killing.

But eventually, in November 1969, the American press got hold of the story from a soldier who had heard rumours of the massacre. Calley, as the officer in charge of one of the platoons, was the only soldier convicted of murder after the investigation. In 1971 he was sentenced to life imprisonment for personally killing 22 villagers. He served less than four years before President Nixon pardoned him and he became a free man.

The killings at My Lai divided the United States. A few were horrified but many were not. Some defended Calley and his men because they were fighting for their country. They believed that the villagers had been helping the Vietcong and that there were VC in the village. In one poll, 49 per cent refused to believe the report at all. In a telephone poll of a thousand people only seven per cent agreed with Calley's sentence.

GOOD GUYS AND BAD GUYS

When photographs of the dead, taken by the army's own photographer (see source D), were published in an American newspaper, there were complaints that the paper was 'rotten and anti-American'. Others claimed that it showed how rotten the war was and that My Lai was just one of many other massacres that nobody knew about. Many believed that the Army should have put on trial Calley's superior officers as well.

Seymour Hersh, the journalist who broke the story, had a lot of trouble finding a newspaper to publish it. Eventually he did and it was quickly picked up by the media across the world. Hersh won the Pulitzer Prize, America's top prize for journalists.

Americans were used to seeing themselves as the 'good guys'. For a generation fed on John Wayne's movie heroics, Americans saw themselves as decent and upright. Some now wondered how true this was if their soldiers were responsible for massacres like My Lai. As for the villagers of My Lai, and many like them; if they weren't VC supporters before the events of 16 March 1968, they were now.

A SOURCE

An American weekly magazine, *Time*, ran this report on My Lai in November 1969.

The brief action at My Lai, a hamlet in Vietcong-infested territory 335 miles northeast of Saigon, may yet have an impact on the war. According to accounts that suddenly appeared on TV and in the world press last week, a company of 60 or 70 US infantrymen had entered My Lai early one morning and destroyed its houses, its livestock and all the inhabitants that they could find in a brutal operation that took less than 20 minutes. When it was over, the Vietnamese dead totalled at least 100 men, women and children, and perhaps many more.

B SOURCE

A modern historian on the My Lai massacre (from *The USA and Vietnam, 1945–75*, V Sanders, 2002).

The most famous but by no means the only example of American hatred of the Vietnamese was the massacre of apparently pro-communist My Lai on March 16 1968. 347 unarmed civilians were beaten and killed by American soldiers and their officers: old men, women, teenagers and even babies. Women were beaten with rifle butts, raped, and shot. Water buffalo, pigs and chickens were shot then dropped in wells to poison the water.

C SOURCE

An account of the My Lai massacre from the website of WGBH Boston, a US radio and TV station.

On March 16 1968 the angry and frustrated men of Charlie Company entered the village of My Lai. My Lai lay in the South Vietnamese district of Son My, a Vietcong area.

As the 'search and destroy' mission unfolded it soon turned into the massacre of over 300 apparently unarmed civilians including women, children, and the elderly. According to eyewitness reports offered after the event, several old men were bayoneted, praying women and children were shot in the back of the head, and at least one girl was raped, and then killed.

D SOURCE

Photograph taken by Ron Haeberle, the official army photographer at My Lai.

E SOURCE

An account of the massacre from some of the My Lai villagers who survived (from *My Lai 4*, S Hersh, 1970).

. . . Le Tong, a 28-year-old rice farmer, reported seeing one woman raped after GIs [US soldiers] killed her children. Nguyen Khoa, a 37-year-old peasant, told of a 13-year-old girl who was raped before being killed. GIs then attacked Khoa's wife, tearing off her clothes. Before they could rape her, however, Khoa said, their six-year-old son, riddled with bullets, fell and saturated her with blood. The GIs left her alone.

F SOURCE

Hugh Thompson being awarded the Soldier's Medal in 1998 for 'heroism above and beyond the call of duty' for his actions at My Lai in 1968.

Questions

a What can you learn from Source A about the events at My Lai?

b Does Source C support the evidence of Sources A and B about the events at My Lai?

c How useful are Sources D and E as evidence about the events at My Lai?

d 'The events at My Lai showed the US army to be bloodthirsty killers.' Use the sources and your own knowledge to explain whether you agree with this view.

12 THE WAR AND CIVIL RIGHTS

Key Issue

- How did the Civil Rights Movement have an impact on the war?

The United States had denied black people in America equal rights and justice since they were first brought to North America as slaves in the seventeenth century. Slavery ended in 1863 but that did not bring justice and equality for America's blacks. The **Civil Rights Movement** began to campaign for the end to segregation and the laws which allowed blacks to be treated as inferior to whites.

Segregation was enforced in many southern US states and meant that blacks and whites were kept apart in public life. For example, white and blacks had their own schools, hotels, restaurants, toilets and even drinking fountains. The facilities which the blacks used were always inferior to those available to the whites.

In the 1950s, blacks began to challenge this inequality and had made some progress in ending segregation in education and transport. In 1948 President Truman ordered the army to be desegregated so that black and white soldiers now served side by side, instead of in separate units.

BLACK INEQUALITY

Fewer blacks had places at university and so it was harder for them to escape the draft. Therefore, in 1967, 30 per cent of black men who were the right age for the draft were conscripted, whereas only 19 per cent of whites were. The government was also worried by the fact that blacks made up 22 per cent of those killed in action and yet they made up only 11 per cent of US forces in Vietnam.

The government tried to get this figure down because it suggested that black troops were deliberately being used in more dangerous combat situations than white ones. In 1970 the statistics for black combat deaths fell to just nine per cent.

However, this came too late to convince civil rights leaders that the government was treating blacks fairly. Another well-known opponent of the war was the world champion boxer, Muhammad Ali. He was conscripted but refused to serve on the grounds that the war was against his Muslim faith. He was stripped of his world title, his passport and banned from boxing.

NATION OF ISLAM

Ali was a member of the Nation of Islam. This group opposed the war because they saw it as a white man's war. The questions these black Muslims asked attracted some support. Why were US blacks travelling 8000 miles across the world to oppress another group of coloured people? Why were they fighting for a country which refused to give them basic human rights? Black opponents of the war were quick to point out that 'the Vietcong never called us nigger'.

MARTIN LUTHER KING

In 1967, Martin Luther King, the best known of black civil rights campaigners, spoke out against the war. A year later, King was assassinated by a white opponent of civil rights and there were race riots in a hundred cities across America.

RACE IN THE FIELD

Inevitably, the racial tensions that existed in the United States were also felt in Vietnam. In the first couple of years of the war, however, there was less racial tension. Most of the soldiers – black and white – were career or professional soldiers and wanted to be in Vietnam. For black soldiers, the army provided a job and an opportunity to earn some respect. In 'the bush' or 'field' (combat zone), black and white soldiers depended on each other to survive and, therefore, they worked together.

However, by 1969, the volunteers had been replaced by black conscripts and attitudes had changed. These men were more interested in their civil rights than they were in fighting a war which they knew was lost.

A SOURCE

A black soldier describing his tour of duty in Vietnam (adapted from *Bloods – An Oral History of the Vietnam War by Black Veterans*, W Terry, 1984).

*There was another guy in our unit who had made it known that he was a card-carrying **Ku Klux Klan** member. That hacked a lot of us off, because the black and white soldiers in our unit had been working really well together. We didn't have racial incidents like what was happening in the rear area, because we had to depend on each other. We were always in the bush.*

B SOURCE

A white soldier on relations between the black and white soldiers (from *Everything We Had – An Oral History of the Vietnam War*, A Santoli, 1981).

The black/white relationship was tense. I saw a couple of fist fights. It usually happened when somebody got mad, and the first thing that happens in an argument between a young white and a black is names start flying and the first word that comes out of the white man's mouth is 'nigger'. And the fists start flying. I saw this happen in the field, as a matter of fact.

C SOURCE

A white soldier commenting on relations between white and black troops (from *A Life in a Year*, J R Ebert, 1993).

Trouble was always seething beneath the surface. But in the bush we needed each other so much that we got along pretty well. The rear was a different story . . . The farther back in the rear you got, the worse it was. And blacks and whites who were friends in the bush felt intimidated or awkward together behind the lines.

D SOURCE

Vietnam veterans join anti-war protestors in a demonstration against the Vietnam War in Washington, 1971.

E SOURCE

Martin Luther King, speaking on the use of black soldiers in the Vietnam War (from an American website).

[The government is] sending their sons and their brothers and their husbands to fight and to die in extraordinarily high proportions relative to the rest of the population ... We have been repeatedly faced with the cruel irony of watching Negro and white boys on TV screens as they kill and die together for a nation that has been unable to seat them together in the same schools.

F SOURCE

A wounded white soldier is helped from the field by a black **GI** in 1968.

Questions

a What can you learn from Source A about relations between black and white soldiers in Vietnam?

b Does Source C support the evidence of Sources A and B about relations between black and white soldiers in Vietnam? Explain your answer.

c How useful are Sources D and E as evidence of attitudes to the war in the United States?

d 'Racism was a major problem among US troops in Vietnam.' Use the sources and your own knowledge to explain whether you agree with this view.

Key Issue

- In what ways did people oppose the Vietnam war?

In Chapter 10 you read how the media began to question the war in 1967. By this date, also, a national movement against the war had developed. Opposition came from a variety of political points of view. Some opponents were socialists or radicals who sympathised with the struggle of the people of Vietnam to create an independent and unified country. Others were **pacifists** who were against the war on moral and religious grounds. They believed that all war is wrong and that this one in particular was against Christian teaching. There were also those who simply felt that Vietnam wasn't worth the lives of young American men.

BURNING DRAFT CARDS

An early form of protest was **draft** card burning. Men who were to be conscripted or drafted into the army received a draft card from one of 4000 draft boards. Some burned their draft orders in public. Others just refused to report for training. Both were criminal offences. By the end of 1969 there were 34,000 **draft-dodgers** wanted by the police. Many crossed the border to Canada to avoid arrest.

MARTIN LUTHER KING

Students were involved in the anti-war movement from the beginning. The Student Non-Violent Coordinating Committee had been set up to campaign for equal rights for blacks, but in 1966 it also began to oppose the war. A year later, in April 1967, the black civil rights leader, Martin Luther King, joined the anti-war movement (see Source A). He was worried that most of the recruits to Vietnam were poor and that a large proportion of the poor were black.

Luther King was disappointed with the failure of President Johnson's 'Great Society' programme. When Johnson won the 1964 election he promised a 'Great Society' in which the poor, and especially blacks, would receive decent welfare payments and decent homes. However, little had been achieved. Although Johnson still wanted these improvements, the govern-

ment couldn't afford both them and the war. The war was costing over $20 billion a year and Johnson had to cut something. The 'Great Society' was put aside for the time being.

JOHNSON QUITS

In March 1968 Johnson announced that he would not stand for re-election as president in November. He realised that the war would cost him any chance of being re-elected. Some would oppose Johnson because they would blame him for not winning the war. Others would oppose him because he was going on with it.

Developments like these encouraged the anti-war movement. Huge protest marches took place in 1969, 1970 and 1971. Perhaps as many as 500,000 took part in the protest in Washington in April 1971. Leading the way were Vietnam Veterans Against the War, among them was the 2004 presidential candidate, John Kerry. Two weeks later there was a demonstration in support of the war. Only 15,000 took part.

KENT STATE

In April 1970 President Nixon, the president who replaced Johnson, announced that United States troops had entered neutral Cambodia. Nixon claimed that this was only to destroy communist

An anti-war demonstration in front of the Pentagon in October 1967. The large placard shows a picture of President Johnson over the words 'war criminal'. Growing opposition to the war helped to convince Johnson that he would not be re-elected as president in 1968.

bases used by the Vietcong. To opponents of the war, it just looked as though another 'Vietnam' was about to begin. Protests took place in universities across the United States at this escalation in their country's role. In one of these protests in May, four students were shot dead by **National Guard** soldiers at Kent State University, Ohio. The killings sparked off 400 protests and strikes in yet more universities.

'OPERATION PHOENIX'

In 1968 the United States **Central Intelligence Agency (CIA)** set up 'Operation Phoenix'. The purpose behind this was to identify and arrest VC suspects in areas controlled by the South Vietnamese government. The CIA set a target of 3000 suspects to be 'neutralised' each month. The idea was to arrest them, get them to talk, reveal other names and then imprison them. In the next three years secret South Vietnamese squads with American advisers captured and imprisoned 28,000 VC suspects. Another 20,000 were assassinated and 17,000 defected – that is, changed sides and supported the South.

A SOURCE

Martin Luther King speaking on the Vietnam War (adapted from *A Testament of Hope*, J R Washington, 1986).

The war has put us in the position of protecting a corrupt government that is stacked against the poor. We are spending $500,000 to kill every Vietcong soldier while we spend only $53 for every person considered to be in poverty in the USA. It has put us in a position of appearing to the world as an arrogant nation. Here we are 10,000 miles away from home fighting for the so-called freedom of the Vietnamese people when we have so much to do in our own country.

B SOURCE

Johnson explaining his reasons for abandoning his Great Society programme (from *Lyndon Johnson and the American Dream*, D Kearns, 1976).

I knew from the start that ... if I abandoned the Great Society in order to get involved with that bitch of a war on the other side of the world, then I would lose everything at home. But if I left that war and let the communists take over South Vietnam, then I would be seen as a coward and my nation would be seen as one which gave in to threats. We would both find it impossible to achieve anything for anybody anywhere on the entire globe.

C SOURCE

A 1972 American cartoon published in the *St Paul Dispatch*, showing Nixon on top of a Christmas tree.

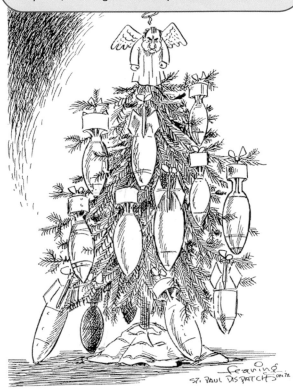

Questions

a Why did President Johnson decide not to stand for re-election in 1968?

b Sources A and B give different views of the Vietnam War. Why do you think they are different? Use Sources A and B and your own knowledge to answer this question.

c How useful is Source C to an historian studying American attitudes to the war? Use Source C and your own knowledge to answer this question.

d Why did opposition to the war increase? You may refer in your answer to:
• News of the My Lai massacre
• Student protests
• Cost of the war.

14 VIETNAMISATION

Key Issue

→ How was a peace agreement achieved?

Nixon won the 1968 presidential election with a narrow majority over his **Democrat** opponent. One of the promises he made during the election campaign was to 'de-Americanise' the war. This suggested that the United States would play a smaller role in the war although Nixon also pledged that the war would go on until 'peace with honour' could be achieved.

Peace talks with North Vietnam had started in Paris in May 1968. No progress had been made. Each side stuck to its position. The biggest difference was that the North would only agree to a peace which reunited both Vietnams. The United States would only agree to a peace which kept South Vietnam as a separate country.

The North also insisted that the **communist** National Liberation Front should form part of a new government in the South. The United States insisted that all North Vietnamese and American forces should leave South Vietnam. Then free elections could take place and the winners could set up a government. The Hanoi government believed that these elections would never be fair and rejected the American terms.

VIETNAMISATION

Nixon and his National Security adviser, Henry Kissinger, wanted a way out of the war without making it look as though the United States had lost. Nguyen Van Thieu had been president of South Vietnam since 1967. He was suspicious of the United States. One of North Vietnam's terms was that Thieu could not be part of any new government of South Vietnam. Thieu was afraid that the Americans might dump him in order to reach an agreement with the North.

Nixon developed a double strategy. He would carry out 'Vietnamisation'. This meant that gradually American troops would leave Vietnam. As they left, the South Vietnamese Army would do more and more of the fighting. The United States would continue to support the Saigon government with the United States Air Force and equipment. At the same time, the peace negotiations in Paris would carry on. If the North refused to change its position, then the United States would increase the bombing raids on North Vietnam until they changed their minds.

There was only a small problem with this strategy. It didn't work. The Hanoi government realised that all it had to do was hang on. The anti-war movement in the United States was getting stronger each day. Eventually, the Americans would pull out of South Vietnam, leaving the South on its own. The **ARVN** would be no match for the communist forces and it would not be long until South Vietnam was reunited with the North.

PEACE AGREEMENT

By October 1972 Kissinger, Nixon's key adviser, and the chief negotiator for North Vietnam, Le Duc Tho, had worked out a settlement. The terms were:

- A ceasefire over all Indo-China
- American troops would withdraw from Vietnam within 60 days of the ceasefire
- American prisoners of war would be freed – there were nearly 700 of these
- Elections would be held in the South to choose a new government
- Each side would stay only in those areas it controlled when the ceasefire started.

Kissinger was keen to get an agreement before Nixon stood for election in November. Nixon wanted a second term of four years as president and a peace agreement would clinch it. It did. Nixon won by a huge majority. Thieu, the leader of South Vietnam, was furious. He believed, correctly, that the terms would leave the South at the mercy of the North. He rejected them. Le Duc Tho broke off further negotiations in December.

On 18 December 1972 Nixon ordered another massive bombing campaign over North Vietnam. In 11 days more bombs were dropped than in the whole of the period 1969–71. As a gesture of Christian goodwill, the bombing was stopped for Christmas Day. The North agreed to re-open negotiations. Nixon told Thieu that if he didn't sign the agreement then the United States would sign it without him. Thieu gave in. The Paris Peace Agreement was signed on 27 January 1973.

A SOURCE

A modern historian describes the situation in South Vietnam in 1973 (adapted from *The Vietnam War, 1956–75*, A Wiest, 2002).

In 1973 the situation looked hopeful for the South Vietnamese. The ARVN (South Vietnamese army) was over one million strong and was equipped with the very latest US weaponry. The communists had only 150,000 troops in South Vietnam. The ARVN was in a dominant position but it was not to last long. The South Vietnamese government was weak and corrupt . . . In 1973 the United States sent $2.3 billion in aid to South Vietnam.

B SOURCE

An overview of the military situation in 1973 is given below (from *The Vietnam War*, R L Bowers, 2000).

The promise of continued American military and economic aid appeared to give the South Vietnamese government a thin hope of long-term survival. Some 145,000 communist troops controlled about one third of the land area of the South. This area contained approximately 5% of the total population of the South.

C SOURCE

A modern historian describes the political situation in Vietnam in 1973 (from *Vietnam – A History*, S Karnow, 1994).

The CIA reported in April 1973 that the North Vietnamese in the South Vietnam numbered roughly 150,000 men. Thieu's government was in good shape at the start of the truce. His army, equipped with last-minute deliveries of American weapons and still receiving US aid, controlled roughly 75% of South Vietnam's territory and about 85% of its population.

Questions

a What can you learn from Source A about the situation in South Vietnam when the peace agreement was signed?

b Does Source C support the evidence of Sources A and B about the situation in South Vietnam when the peace agreement was signed?

c How useful are Sources D and E as evidence of the success of Nixon's policy in Vietnam?

d 'Nixon's policy in Vietnam was a success.' Use the sources and your own knowledge to explain whether you agree with this view.

D SOURCE

An American cartoon from the *Hartford Times*, 1972.

E SOURCE

An American pilot is greeted by his family after being released from a North Vietnamese prison camp in February 1973.

F SOURCE

A history book on the peace agreement (from *A Concise History of the American Republic*, S E Morison, H S Commager, W E Leuchtenburg, 1983) said the following about the peace.

Nixon boasted that he had achieved 'peace with honour'. In fact, the peace agreement reflected an absolute defeat and the term 'honour' was totally irrelevant. The war had cost 57,000 American lives, more than 300,000 wounded say; had inflicted over one million casualties on the Vietnamese; had cost billions of dollars.

15 REASONS FOR THE US DEFEAT

Key Issue

• Why did the United States lose?

HEARTS AND MINDS

The Americans had realised from an early stage that the war could only be won by winning the support of the South Vietnamese peasants. This policy was called winning the 'hearts and minds' of the people. The problem was that the Americans didn't know how to do it and the rulers of South Vietnam didn't want to do it.

The key issue was land reform. The VC made sure that in areas under their control land was taken from the rich landowners and given to the poor peasants. This was very popular. Rulers of South Vietnam like Diem and Thieu would not carry out this policy and the Americans would not force them.

The Americans became more and more frustrated with their failure to break the support of the peasants for the VC. They tried the strategic hamlet programme (see pages 10–11) but that just caused even more resentment. In the end the Americans relied on purely military methods. They became frustrated because they couldn't tell VC supporters from ordinary villagers. This led to massacres like My Lai and increased the peasants' hatred.

TACTICS

The VC and NVA military strategy was as successful as their political one. They knew they couldn't match the massive fire-power of the United States forces. So, they avoided large-scale battles and adopted **guerrilla** tactics instead. This wore down the American and **ARVN** forces, which suffered casualties often without even catching a glimpse of their communist enemy.

The NVA and VC forces were never as well supplied or as well equipped as their opponents – not until after 1973, anyway. But the Chinese and the Soviet Union provided enough weapons and supplies to keep the North Vietnamese going. Especially valuable were Soviet anti-aircraft guns, and missiles. Towards the end of the war Soviet tanks were important too.

MORALE

Eventually, what really mattered was morale. The **communist** forces were much more committed to their cause and they fought with a real desire to win. The South Vietnamese Army was never a match in morale or fighting ability for the NVA and VC. The Americans could match the fighting ability of their enemies but they didn't have the same belief in their cause.

'Fragging' and drug abuse are examples of what happens to an army that has lost its way. News of the growing opposition movement to the war in the United States also undermined the troops' morale. This opposition was a big factor, too, in forcing an American withdrawal.

OPPOSITION IN THE US

But the war was not lost for military reasons alone. Politics played a big part, too. A key factor in forcing the US out of the war was the strength of the peace movement in the United States. The war, which clearly could not be won, had become very unpopular. Nixon knew that continuing the war would cost him any chance of being re-elected president in 1972. His decision to pull the US out was a vote-winner in 1972.

A SOURCE

An historian on why the United States lost the war (from *Guerrilla Warfare*, R Corbett, 1986).

The leadership of South Vietnam was hopelessly corrupt and inefficient. Only American support could keep the country in existence for long. The North Vietnamese Army had superb morale and discipline, excellent leadership from the lowest to the highest levels.

B SOURCE

An historian on why the United States lost the war (from *The USA and Vietnam, 1945–75*, V Sanders, 2002).

The communists fought with incredible determination. The guerrillas were never going to give up. The Americans fought a limited war in which their tactics only made the communists more popular. Their South Vietnamese allies were usually corrupt, inefficient and unpopular ... the morale of the American army fell from 1968 onwards.

C SOURCE

A modern historian on why the United States lost the war (adapted from *America and the Vietnam War*, G J DeGroot, 2000).

Defeat was inevitable not because the Americans used the wrong strategy, but because America backed an ally which had no future in Vietnam. The government of South Vietnam was corrupt and cruel. The US was not only weighed down by a weak ally, it also faced a very strong enemy. The VC were not a bunch of barefoot guerrillas but a highly trained, fiercely determined and well armed fighting force which was at its best in small unit actions.

D SOURCE

Anti-war demonstrators in Washington, 1969.

E SOURCE

A Vietnam veteran on why the United States lost the war (from *Everything We Had – An Oral History of the Vietnam War*, A Santoli, 1981).

I think the North Vietnamese played us better than we know. They just totally out-psyched us. We lost the war because of will, not military, power. I think they initially looked at Tet in 1968 as a disaster, but our reaction in the United States was so over-whelming – I mean, it toppled the President – that all of a sudden it became clear to them that they could make the Americans beat themselves.

F SOURCE

Children fleeing from their village after it had been bombed with napalm by US jets, 1972.

Questions

a What can you learn from Source A about why the United States lost the war?

b Does Source C support the evidence of Sources A and B about why the United States lost the war?

c How useful are Sources D and E as evidence about why the United States lost the war?

d 'The Americans lost the war in Vietnam because they lacked the will to win.' Use the sources and your own knowledge to explain whether you agree with this view.

16 VIETNAM UNITED

Key Issue

- What happened after the Americans left?

THE COLLAPSE OF SOUTH VIETNAM

The fighting between the **communists** and the South Vietnamese army quickly started again in 1973 as expected. At first, Thieu's forces held their own, but in 1974 low morale and poor leadership weakened their commitment. In April 1975, the NVA forces entered Saigon. Thieu fled the country to live in Britain. Several hundred thousand South Vietnamese who also had reason to fear the communists were not so lucky. The last 6000 Americans to leave Vietnam were lifted out of Saigon by helicopter on 30 April 1975. They left behind scenes of civilian panic.

But the war, which for the people of Vietnam had started back in 1941 against the Japanese, was finally over. North and South Vietnam were reunited. Saigon, now renamed Ho Chi Minh City, was declared as its capital city.

POST-WAR VIETNAM

Both Americans and South Vietnamese had expected a bloodbath as the communists were expected to take their revenge on those South Vietnamese who had worked with the Americans. Some 60,000 were executed but most of the supporters of the old government, about 300,000 people, were sent to camps to be 're-educated'.

Many more people of the South tried desperately to escape the economic policies of their new communist rulers. The communists took their land and their animals. Between 1975 and 1990 perhaps as many as 1.5 million escaped by sea to what they hoped would be a better life. These 'boat people' often found worse conditions in refugee camps. Some were sent back to Vietnam; about a million were able to settle in France and the United States where they had to rebuild their lives from the bottom of society. Probably at least 50,000 of these refugees drowned or were murdered by pirates.

US CHEMICAL WARFARE

For those who stayed behind, there were further problems. The Americans had waged a nine-year chemical warfare campaign against the forests and countryside of South Vietnam. The chemicals used by the Americans in Agent Orange to destroy vegetation and foliage have caused a high level of cancer among the South Vietnamese and the birth of many deformed children. The areas sprayed with Agent Orange still cannot grow anything.

Two thousand Vietnamese have been killed and wounded trying to clear away the estimated 17 million unexploded munitions – artillery shells, mines and bombs which the war left behind.

For more than 20 years after the war, Vietnam was one of the world's poorest countries, partly because of its own communist economic policies and partly because of the devastation which almost 40 years of wars had caused. The ending of aid from the Soviet Union in 1991 forced the rulers of Vietnam to change policies. In recent years, private businesses have been allowed and there is less poverty than there was during the 1970s and 1980s.

FURTHER CONFLICT

Despite the support which communist China had given North Vietnam during its war with the US, relations with China – a traditional enemy of the Vietnamese – became strained after the war was over. The Vietnamese began to treat harshly those Vietnamese of Chinese origin who lived in Vietnam. This angered China, and relations got sharply worse after 1978 when the Vietnamese invaded Cambodia and overthrew the pro-Chinese communist government of Pol Pot. China was concerned by this growth in Vietnamese influence in the region. China's answer was to invade Vietnam in early 1979.

The Chinese suffered heavy casualties in the brief conflict. But they had made it clear that they would not tolerate Vietnamese aggression in the region. In 1989 the Vietnamese ended their occupation of Cambodia and relations with China (and the US) began to improve.

A SOURCE

In 1990 South Vietnam's former ruler, Nguyen Van Thieu, was interviewed by the American weekly magazine, *Time*, about his policies if he returned to Vietnam.

Interviewer: 'You say that you want a multiparty democracy. But Vietnam does not have a tradition of democracy and did not when you were in power.'

Thieu: 'That is not true. Vietnam has had a strong democratic tradition for centuries. Under my regime, even in wartime, we applied democracy in a Western style by having not only an elected national assembly and provincial councils but also at the hamlet and village level.'

B SOURCE

A modern historian on Thieu's rule while he was in power in South Vietnam (from *The USA and Vietnam, 1945–75*, V Sanders, 2002).

In 1971 Congress questioned President Nixon about 'his' undemocratic ally (Thieu). President Johnson's plan for South Vietnam had called for a presidential election for October 1971. Thieu held it, but allowed only one candidate – himself! Some senators tried to halt all aid to South Vietnam unless there was a democratic election. Nixon could only say that democracy took time to develop.

Questions

a How justified were the fears of some South Vietnamese that the communists would take bloody revenge against their enemies after they took over in 1975?

b Sources A and B give different views of Thieu's rule. Why do you think they are different? Use Sources A and B and your own knowledge to answer this question.

c How useful is Source C to an historian studying economic conditions in Vietnam in 1990? Use Source C and your own knowledge to answer this question.

d Why has the war continued to affect the people of Vietnam? You may refer in your answer to:
  • 'The boat people'
  • Effects of chemical warfare and munitions
  • Economic problems.

C SOURCE

South Vietnamese traders returning from China with consumer goods to sell in Vietnam.

Key Issue

- What impact did the war have on the US?

AMERICA AND THE WAR

The war has cast a long shadow over the United States. The most immediate effect of the war was that President Johnson's ambitious 'Great Society' programme had to be abandoned. The cost of the war was too great to spend money on improved welfare. This meant that many of America's severe social problems – poverty, slums, lack of medical care for the poor, racial inequalities – could not be tackled.

The war led to limits being placed on the power of the president. The War Powers Act of 1973 stated that the president had to get the approval of Congress to use combat troops abroad for any longer than three months.

The war bitterly divided the nation and caused protests and political conflict between supporters and opponents. It ruined Johnson's chances of being re-elected president in 1968 and even became an issue in the presidential election campaign in 2004. The **Democratic** candidate, John Kerry, was a decorated Vietnam veteran who later turned against the war, while President George W Bush had avoided Vietnam by serving in the **National Guard** in the United States.

The 1982 memorial to America's Vietnam War dead. All 58,000 names are recorded on these granite walls.

THE VIETNAM SYNDROME

The long-term effects of the war have been just as important. For a long time the United States was determined to avoid fighting another 'Vietnam'. This meant that the Americans refused to send troops into any conflict which did not directly affect the United States' own security. This was known as the Nixon Doctrine. As a result, the United States did little to challenge directly the Soviet Union's actions in other countries such as Afghanistan and Angola. They were worried that American troops might get sucked into the conflict, as they had in Vietnam.

Eventually this concern that every international crisis was a potential Vietnam for the United States became less of a worry. Their decisive and speedy victories in the 1991 Gulf War and against Iraq in 2003 ended the 'Vietnam Syndrome'. It allowed Americans to believe now that they could fight a war, win it quickly and with very few casualties.

VETERANS

Of its three million veterans, 500,000 suffered the effects of post-traumatic stress disorder; among its features are panic and rage attacks, depression, drug addiction, divorce, and suicide. More American veterans have committed suicide since the war than were killed in the war itself. For them, the process of adjusting to peacetime was too difficult. Many of them felt betrayed by a country which they felt was embarrassed by them.

It wasn't until 1982 that a memorial was built (see opposite) – paid for by private individuals – to commemorate America's 58,000 killed in action. Each of their names is cut into three black granite blocks. To some, the memorial did not adequately portray the heroism and sacrifice of those killed and so another memorial was added of three soldiers in bronze in 1984.

THE END

In 1985 an American veteran, William Ehrhart, went back to Vietnam. There he spoke to a North Vietnamese general.

'Would it have mattered if we had done things differently?' Ehrhart asked.

'No,' the general replied after a pause. 'Probably not. History was not on your side. We were fighting for our homeland. What were you fighting for?'

Ehrhart answered, 'Nothing that really mattered.'

A SOURCE

A Vietnam veteran, David Donovan, writing about the Vietnam War (from *Once a Warrior King*, D Donovan, 1985).

We were right to resist terror and war being inflicted on a poor and backward people ... I maintain in the face of all accusers that we who served did so when our only thought was duty and our only cause was freedom. I do not accept any guilt about an 'immoral' war at all. It was a decent cause gone terribly wrong. I hold the cause of the South Vietnamese people in my heart. I yearned for their freedom; I fought for it with them.

B SOURCE

A black American veteran remembers the war (from *Bloods – An Oral History of the Vietnam War by Black Veterans*, W Terry, 1984).

Vietnam taught you to be a liar. To be dishonest. You weren't there for democracy. You weren't protecting your homeland. I think we were the last generation to believe, you know, in the honour of war. There is no honour in war. My mama still thinks that I did my part for my country, because she's a very patriotic person. I don't.

C SOURCE

A black American veteran remembers the war (from *Bloods – An Oral History of the Vietnam War by Black Veterans*, W Terry, 1984).

I made a promise in 'Nam that I would never risk my life or limb to protect anybody else's property. I will protect my own. So this country is not going to tell me to go out again to stop the spread of communism. If another war breaks out and they want me to go, I'd rather die. I'll fight anyone here in America. But if they come and get me to send me to some other country, I'm going to have my gun ready for them.

The Three Servicemen Memorial bronze sculpture to those who served in Vietnam.

E SOURCE

A Vietnam veteran, David Donovan, describes the veterans' parade in Washington in 1982 at the opening of the memorial (from *Once a Warrior King*, D Donovan, 1985).

The sidewalks were crammed with cheering people. Since I was on the outside of the front rank, people reached out to shake my hand and slap my back. Men, women, and children were cheering and waving flags. The most common cheer was 'Welcome home! Welcome home!' The tears kept filling my eyes, but this time not from sadness – it was from pleasure and immense relief.

F SOURCE

A Vietnam veteran commenting on the war in 2000 (from the *New York Times* website).

I did two tours in Vietnam from 1968 to 1969. It was one hell of an experience, good and bad, which I wouldn't trade for anything . . . Vietnam proved that we were willing to sacrifice our youth in a small backward country halfway around the world to fight the enemy. We lost that battle but won the war [the Cold War].

Questions

a What can you learn from Source A about this veteran's attitude to the war in Vietnam?

b Does Source C support the evidence of Sources A and B about the attitudes of veterans to the war?

c How useful are Sources D and E as evidence about the attitude of the American people to the war?

d 'American veterans think the war was a worthwhile cause.' Use the sources and your own knowledge to explain whether you agree with this view.

The use of the correct *technique* is the key to success in source evaluation papers and this counts for much more than the application of knowledge. The best way to improve this technique, as for any skill, is practice. A key point to remember with the questions on this paper is that how much you write should be directly related to the number of marks available.

EDEXCEL

The sources on which these examples are based are on pages 28–29 of this book.

(a) What can you learn from Source A about the events at My Lai? (4)

TECHNIQUE

- To get more than 2 marks for this question you must read between the lines and make an inference, i.e. write something that the source *suggests* or *implies*.
- A couple of inferences with some explanation will be enough for 4 marks.
- It is a good idea to start your answer with the same phrase each time, i.e 'Source A suggests . . .' or 'Source A implies . . .'

Example: *Source A implies that the US soldiers massacred inhabitants indiscriminately and that, because the story was seen all over the world, this would bring bad publicity for the United States. It was expected that support for the war could fall.*

(b) Does Source C support the evidence of Sources A and B about the events at My Lai? (6)

TECHNIQUE

- It is also essential (for 5/6 marks) to discuss *the extent* to which the sources agree. Do this in a concluding sentence or sentences.
- Do not compare Source A with B. You will get no credit for this.
- Do not comment on whether the sources are reliable or who wrote them. You will get no credit for this.
- Compare Source C with A then C with B. Do not compare C with A and B *together*.

Example: *Source C states that there was a massacre of 'over 300 apparently unarmed civilians' and this is supported by B where it speaks of '347 unarmed civilians were beaten and killed', though B does also mention the killing of livestock which is not referred to in Source C. However, Source A isn't quite so certain as to the numbers of those killed ('at least 100 men, women, and children'). Source C also refers to 'at least one rape' and Source B confirms that there were rapes but Source A does not mention this at all.*

On balance, Source C mostly supports the evidence of Source B but there is much less agreement with Source A.

Note the use of appropriate connectives: 'However', 'though', 'On balance'.

(c) How useful are Sources D and E as evidence about events at My Lai? (8)

TECHNIQUE

- It is essential in this question to write about the *type*, **provenance** or *purpose* of the sources if you are to get more than 6 marks, i.e. achieve a Level 3 response.
- You don't have to comment on all three of these to get to Level 3.
- All of the sources in this question will be useful for something.
- A source is still useful, even if it isn't reliable.
- It is also worth remembering that anyone can build a website – some represent trustworthy sources, for example, the BBC or the *New York Times*, but others may not.

Example, writing about Source D you could say: *Source D is useful because it shows that women and children were killed at My Lai and this confirms the brutal behaviour of the US soldiers. The fact that the photograph was taken by an official US army photographer adds to its usefulness because we have no reason to doubt it is true. If the photo had been taken by the VC of an alleged US massacre, few in the US would have believed it.*

(d) 'The events at My Lai showed the US army to be bloodthirsty killers.' Use the sources and your own knowledge to explain whether you agree with this view. (12)

TECHNIQUE

- It is not generally a good idea to go through the sources one by one, from A to F.
- Group the sources into those which support the point of view of the question and those which do not. Then discuss them.
- You don't have to comment on all the sources to get high marks but three is a minimum.
- You must use both sources and your own knowledge; otherwise you will lose half of the marks available.
- You must finish with a conclusion which makes clear what your judgement of the question is. There isn't a right or wrong answer to this question – you just need to support it with appropriate use of the evidence.

Example conclusion: *In conclusion, the sources mostly support the point of view of the question and so does my own knowledge. Sources A, B, and C all refer to the massacre of women and children. However, we also know that not all the soldiers present at My Lai took part and some tried to stop it. One of these was later decorated for this (Source F). So, it wouldn't be true to say that all those present were 'bloodthirsty killers'.*

AQA

The sources on which these examples are based are on pages 32–33.

(a) Why did President Johnson decide not stand for re-election in 1968? (6)

TECHNIQUE

- A one-reason answer – even if you explain it in detail – won't get you to Level 3 (5/6 marks).
- What is needed here is an answer with several reasons, each explained in some detail.
- Also try to have separate paragraphs for each reason and then link the paragraphs together.

Example: *Johnson decided not to stand for re-election because it was clear that the American public was turning more and more against a war which many now believed the US could not win. The Tet Offensive had a deep effect on public opinion – even if the war could be won, it would take many years of more American deaths. Johnson calculated that he could not win the presidential election in this situation.*

However, there were more than just political reasons for his decision. Johnson had been forced to abandon his Great Society programme to pay for the war and many Americans remained poor or without proper medical care. These people were bitter that they had been sacrificed for the war and Johnson knew he had lost their support.

Note how one paragraph deals with a political reason and how it is linked to the paragraph which deals with an economic reason.

(b) Sources A and B give different views of the Vietnam War. Why do you think they are different? Use Sources A and B and your own knowledge to answer this question. (8)

TECHNIQUE

The key here is to make sure you analyse the sources:

- Discuss the content of the sources (what the sources say).
- Discuss the provenance of the sources; it is also worth remembering that anyone can build a website – some represent trustworthy sources, for example, the BBC or the *New York Times*, but others may not.

- Use some of your own knowledge to support your argument.
- Finish with a clear judgement as to why the sources are different.

Example conclusion: *In conclusion, it is clear that Johnson, as president during the war, would defend his policy of abandoning the Great Society to pay for the war. Martin Luther King, on the other hand, represented the kind of people who felt abandoned by Johnson – the poor blacks of the United States. Clearly, then, King was bound to criticise that war as much as Johnson was bound to defend it.*

(c) How useful is Source C to an historian studying American attitudes towards the war? Use Source C and your own knowledge to answer this question. (8)

TECHNIQUE

- To get beyond Level 1 (1/2 marks) you must consider the provenance of the source.
- Avoid rote-learned responses, for example, 'this is a photograph, therefore it is reliable'.
- Try to comment on the motive behind the photographer or author – what do you think he or she wanted the audience to think?
- A source is still useful even if it isn't reliable.
- How typical is this source, i.e. are there others which support its point of view; does it fit in with your own knowledge?
- Sources are always useful for something.
- Consider the limitations of the source – was the view it expresses widely shared?

Example: *This source is useful because it is an example of the media's opposition to Nixon's policy in Vietnam. It shows Nixon as a scowling angel about to drop more bombs on the Vietnamese. This attitude is typical of much of the media's view of Nixon and the war and this adds to its reliability.*

Indeed, it was a newspaper which was eventually responsible for forcing Nixon to resign in 1974.

However, it is more difficult to be sure whether this view of Nixon was shared by much of the population. We need to know, for example, how many people read the St Paul Dispatch. *As a newspaper, it wasn't as influential as the* New York Times, *for example, and this would limit its usefulness.*

Note that the provenance of the source is discussed in detail as are its typicality, limitations, and content. There is also own knowledge present. However, this answer needs a conclusion to round it off.

(d) Why did opposition to the war increase? You may refer in your answer to:
 - News of My Lai massacre
 - Student protests
 - Cost of the war.
 (8)

TECHNIQUE

- The answer to this question involves the same techniques as for *(a)* – except that it needs to be a longer response.
- The bullets points are there to provide a framework for your answer but you should also use other material if it's relevant.
- You must finish with a reasoned judgement – that is, a clear point of view which reflects the arguments you have used.

Example conclusion: *On balance, Americans opposed the war for different reasons. Some thought it was immoral, others a waste of young American lives and money. Possibly, the most important reason was because it was a war America was losing and, therefore, seemed to serve no purpose at all.*

GLOSSARY

ARVN – Army of the Republic of Vietnam, i.e. the South Vietnamese Army

CIA – the United States' Central Intelligence Agency, which deals with top-secret issues of security

Civil Rights Movement – the movement which campaigns for equal rights and justice for American blacks

Civil war – a war fought between the people of the same country against each other

Cold War – the state of tension (but not actual war) that existed between the Soviet Union and the United States from the late 1940s to the late 1980s.

Colonial power – a country which has control over a group of countries, for example, France over Indo-China

Communist – someone who believes that the workers and peasants should control the country and that it should be free from foreign rule

Congress – the United States' equivalent of Britain's Parliament; Congress has to approve the president's proposals before they can become law

Conscription – the compulsory recruitment of men, and sometimes women, into the armed forces

Coup d'état – commonly called a 'coup': the overthrow of the government by a small group of plotters, very often inside the army

Democrat – a member of the US Democratic Party; also someone who believes in the right of the people to elect their own government

Desertion – running away from the army to avoid combat

Domino theory – the idea that communism was spreading throughout South East Asia, each country falling to communism like a row of dominoes falling over. Each one that fell knocked the next one over, and so on

Draft – an American term describing the compulsory recruitment of men into the armed forces

Draft-dodgers – someone who avoids the draft by, for example, leaving the country and going into hiding

Empire – a group of colonies under the control of another country

GI – stands for General Issue and has come to mean an American soldier

Guerrilla – a type of soldier who uses hit-and-run tactics against the enemy and generally does not wear a uniform; these tactics are often used by weaker forces against a more powerful opponent in what is called a guerilla war

Ideology – a set of political beliefs such as communism or democracy

Korean War (1950–53) – fought between communist North Korea (which was supported by communist China and the Soviet Union) and South Korea and its American allies

Ku Klux Klan – an extreme racist organisation that is against blacks, Catholics, and Jews

Napalm – an explosive petroleum-based jelly used in bombs that sticks to the skin and burns at 800 degrees

National guard – a part-time military force, based in the US, which men could join instead of going to Vietnam

Nationalist – someone who wants to free their country from foreign control and make it fully independent. Nationalists can also want to see their country dominate others

Pacifist – someone opposed to war and the use of violence in general

Patriotism – passionate support for one's own country and a willingness to defend it

Propaganda – methods used to persuade people to believe certain ideas or behave in a certain way; sometimes involves the use of deliberate lies

Provenance – the provenance of a source is about who wrote it and when. Is there anything in the writer's background that makes his or her views more or less reliable? It is important for historians to know a source's provenance to help decide its reliability and value

Puppet – an individual or country controlled by another more powerful individual or country

Republican – member of the US Republican Party. Also someone who is opposed to the idea of a monarch ruling the country

The publishers would like to thank the following individuals, institutions and companies for permission to reproduce copyright illustrations in this book:
Colorific p3; Robert Hunt Library p5; Bettman/Corbis p7; Corbis p8; Bettman/Corbis p9; Hulton Archive/Getty Images p11t; Bettman/Corbis p11b & p13; Associated Press p14; Bettman/Corbis p15; Don McCullin/Contact/nbpictures p17; Hulton Archive/Getty Images p19t; Corbis p19b; Philip Jones Griffiths/Magnum p21l; Don McCullin/Contact/nbpictures p21r; Marc Riboud/Magnum p23; Popperphoto p25; Corbis p26; Associated Press p27; Ronald L Haeberle p29l; Sipa Press/Rex Features p29r; Hulton Archive/Getty Images p31l; Bettman/Corbis p31r; Corbis p33l; St Paul Despatch/Fearing p33r; Hartford Times p35t; Sal Veder/Associated Press p35b; Bettman/Corbis p37 l&r; Vittoriano Rastelli/Corbis p39; author's own p40 & 42.

The publishers would also like to thank the following for permission to reproduce material in this book:
Abacus, *The Bloody Game* by P Fussell; Appleton Century Crofts, *Documents of American History* by H S Commager; Ballantine Books, *Bloods* by W Terry & *Everything We Had* by A Santoli & *Lyndon: An Oral Biography* by M Miller; Bison Books, *Atlas of the Twentieth Century* by R Natkiel; Corgi, *Once A Warrior King: Memories of an Officer in Vietnam* by D Donovan; Harper Collins, *The Collins History of the World* by J A S Grenville & *Lyndon Johnson and the American Dream* by D Kearns; Hodder, *The USA and Vietnam* by V Sanders; I B Tauris, *Vietnam – A Portrait of its People at War* by D Chanoff & D Van Thoai; Longman, *America and the Vietnam War* by G J DeGroot; Orbis, *Guerrilla Warfare: From 1939 to the Present Day* by R Corbett; Osprey, *The Vietnam War 1956–75* by A Wiest; Oxford University Press, *A Concise History of the American Republic* by S E Morison, *et al*; Picador, *A Bright Shining Lie* by N Sheehan; Pimlico, *Vietnam – A History* by S Karnow; Presido, *A Life in a Year* by J R Ebert; Salamander Books, *The Vietnam War* by R L Bowers; *Time* magazine.

Every effort has been made to trace and acknowledge ownership of copyright. The publishers will be glad to make suitable arrangements with any copyright holders whom it has not been possible to contact.

Note about the Internet links in the book. The user should be aware that URLs or web addresses change regularly. Every effort has been made to ensure the accuracy of the URLs provided in this book on going to press. It is inevitable, however, that some will change. It is sometimes possible to find a relocated web page, by just typing in the address of the home page for a website in the URL window of your browser.

Orders: please contact Bookpoint Ltd, 130 Milton Park, Abingdon, Oxon OX14 4SB. Telephone: (44) 01235 827720. Fax: (44) 01235 400454. Lines are open from 9.00 – 5.00, Monday to Saturday, with a 24 hour message answering service. You can also order through our website www.hoddereducation.co.uk.

British Library Cataloguing in Publication Data
A catalogue record for this title is available from the British Library

ISBN-10: 0 340 81475 6
ISBN-13: 978 0 340 81475 8

First Published 2004
Impression number   10 9 8 7 6 5 4
Year   2010 2009 2008 2007 2006

Copyright © Neil DeMarco 2004.

Cover photo from Tim Page/Corbis.
Typeset by Fakenham Photosetting Limited, Fakenham, Norfolk. Artwork on p2, 5, 6 and 25 by Art Construction.
Printed in Italy for Hodder Murray, an imprint of Hodder Education, a member of the Hodder Headline Group, 338 Euston Road, London NW1 3BH